# Hellfire in Hermantown

## The 1918 Forest Fires and How They Affected Hermantown

Savage PRESS
14172 E Carlson Rd. • Brule, WI 54820
(218) 391-3070 • www.savpress.com

# Hellfire in Hermantown

## The 1918 Forest Fires and How They Affected Hermantown

Connie Jacobson

First Edition



Cover Artist: Karen Holden
Cover Design: Dezime Graphics



ISBN: 978-1-937706-18-0

Library of Congress Catalog Number: 2017964674

Published by:
Savage Press
14172 E Carlson Rd.
Brule, WI 54820
Email: mail@savpress.com
Website: www.savpress.com
Printed in the United States of America

# TABLE OF CONTENTS

# Dedication

This book is dedicated to the memory all those brave souls in the Township of Herman who perished as well as those who lived through the Fires of October 12, 1918, including my parents, Helmer and Evelyn (Witte) Jacobson. They all deserve to be remembered with much honor and respect.

# PREFATORY REMARKS

October 12, 2018, marks the 100th year since the deadly Fires of 1918. Commemorative programs and events have been scheduled during all of 2018, in several of the Counties devastated by the Fires. While a few books have been written about the Fires in their entirety, none have been written centering on the Township of Herman. The personal stories of people from various areas, specifically Moose Lake and environs, have been preserved in publications, thanks to the work of the Moose Lake Historical Society. The Carlton County Historical Society has several publications focusing on the 1918 Fires in Cloquet. Other Historical Societies have included chapters about the 1918 Fires in their publications about the history of their communities.

I have always had a personal interest in the Fires of 1918, having heard about them from my parents, grandparents, and their friends. Both of my parents and many other relatives survived the Fires, while a great-great grandfather perished.

The people of Hermantown needed to have their accounts related and preserved for future generations. It is my attempt to extend to them the respect, honor, and reverence they deserve. These writings commemorate their lives before, during, and after the 1918 Fires.

The first portion of this book will describe the conditions that contributed to the explosive 1918 Fires. To capture the magnitude of the catastrophe certain technical descriptions are included to expand the reader's understanding of fires and the scars they leave in their aftermath.

The second section of the book contains the memoirs of the survivors, stories from their descendants and information taken from newspapers of the day. It is also a section where I become a narrator of my family's stories, those of my family's neighbors, and those of a number of Hermantown contributors sharing their family's history of the fires.

As with all catastrophes there are always questions as to why it happened and what the impact was. With this catastrophe the questions have been answered. What remains are the stories. They are accounts of loss, hope, sadness, joy, heroism, sacrifice, and countless other expressions of the human experience. Some of those stories are found here.

# Part One: General Fire Information

## Chapter One: Endless Forests

The settlers' attitudes toward forests and fire appear to have played a part in the tragic forest fires of the late 19th and early 20th centuries in Minnesota.

Forests were seen as an obstacle standing in the way of farming to many of the first settlers of Minnesota. Trees were all too often regarded as only a byproduct of land clearing and as a building material. The timber not needed for building structures was often destroyed by burning.

The early loggers were only interested in large white pine, Norway pine, and then hardwoods. The cutover lands were often purposely burned to protect the remaining stands of timber from wildfire. All too often these controlled fires destroyed sources of seed and future growth. Few, if any people, were concerned about destroying forests; they were seen as being limitless. "The pioneer attitude was that getting rid of the forest meant development," observed Elizabeth Bachmann in her writings about the history of forestry.[1] Even as late as 1880, as an article in the December 24, 1880, *St. Paul and Minneapolis Pioneer Press* stated, the forests were regarded as virtually inexhaustible. "Not one-hundredth part of it ever has been, or will be, required by the lumbermen who annually infest the region to carry on the process of denuding the pine forests." [2]

As a result of that attitude, careless harvesting processes were used. Trees were cut down as quickly as possible with little regard for future timber supplies. Because mature trees were felled so they could be easily retrieved, they fell upon and often damaged or crushed the young growth below them.

The tree tops and branches that were trimmed from the tree trunks, in addition to the brush cut to facilitate the transport of the logs, were carelessly left scattered about with adjacent growth in piles that dried and provided a source of easily ignited fuel for wild fires during dry spells. Whether the waste wood was burned deliberately or accidentally, the humus and ground cover was destroyed, preventing absorption of rain and snow.[3]

The first great conflagration in Minnesota occurred in Hinckley on September 1, 1894. With a death count of 418 and massive destruction of the entire area, changes in attitudes toward logging and fire slowly started to change. When the Minnesota State Legislature met in 1895 General C. C. Andrews used the Hinckley Fire as a major part in the appeal for the public control of forests, for better fire protection, and for restoration of the forests by careful use. He was largely

1 Elizabeth Bachmann, "A History of Forestry in Minnesota," 1965.(files.dnr.state.mn.us/forestry/anniversary.)

2 *Ibid.*, page 6.

3 www.foresthistory.org/ASPNET/Publications/region/8/history/chap1.aspx

responsible for drafting a bill that provided for the creation of a forest commission to enforce the few fire prevention laws in existence.

However, the legislature was pinching pennies and passed a mostly symbolic bill. The state auditor was named forest commissioner and given the authority to appoint a deputy with the title of chief fire warden who would be empowered to enforce the law they passed "for the preservation of forests of this state and for the prevention and suppression of forest and prairie fires." No salary increase was given to the state auditor for his increased duties, but the chief fire warden was awarded a salary of $1,200 per year.[4] Along with various other provisions, the law made supervisors of towns, mayors of cities, and presidents of village councils fire wardens, with the authority to act to prevent and suppress fires in their respective jurisdictions at the salary of $2 per day, not to exceed ten days' service in any given year. Any person employed by the local fire wardens could not be paid for more than five days of fire prevention services a year. Railroad companies were required to equip all their engines with spark arresters, as well as to keep their rights of ways free of combustible materials.[5] With the exception of the chief fire warden, no funds were provided for permanent employees. Township fire wardens were paid only when they actually fought fires.[6]

However, enforcement of the law was all too often lax or non-existent. The many miles of logging railroads were frequently dotted with fires set by the combustible material strewn along their right of way, which the railroads did not clean up.The logging railroads weren't in a hurry to place spark arresters on their engines either. Quite a few Minnesotans seemed to think the forestry laws of 1895 were too severe a reaction to the Hinckley Fire of the previous year. The Minnesota Legislature attempted to repeal the 1895 Act two years after it was enacted.

Throughout the early years of the 20th century various minor protective measures were enacted, with little resources allotted to implement them. Although Minnesotans had become aware of the dangers of fires, many deliberately ignored the fire prevention laws. Few convictions of law breakers were made because the local fire wardens were reluctant to prosecute their own neighbors.[7]

The entire village of Chisholm was almost destroyed by a forest fire on September 4th, 1908. A strong wind brought the fire into the village, which set carelessly discarded slashings ablaze within the Chisholm limits. ('Slashings' or 'slash' is defined in lumbering terms as coarse and fine woody debris generated during logging operations.) [8] Again the following year the legislature attempted to strengthen forest prevention laws, and succeeded to an extent. One notable provision required railroad companies to maintain patrols on their rights of way through countryside liable to be easily set afire.[9]

On October 9, 1910, small fires that had been burning and smoldering during the record dry and hot summer and fall were fanned by a gusty wind into a horrific wildfire. That day the towns of Baudette and Spooner on the Rainey River were annihilated. Although the death toll was 42, it would have been substantially higher had hundreds of people not been saved by trains.[10]

Again the Minnesota legislature responded the following year to strengthen the state fire laws. The Minnesota Forest Service was established in 1911, with the goal of prevention and suppressing fires such as those that destroyed Hinckley, Chisholm, Baudette, and Spooner. Continuing with short sighted precedence to fund forestry and fire legislation, insufficient funds were allocated to accomplish this aim. Conservationist General C. C. Andrews' sound recommendations were not taken. His ideas were determined to be too liberal in scope, and a different and weaker bill was considered.[11]

---

4 Elizabeth Bachmann, "A History of Forestry in Minnesota," 1965. (files.dnr.state.mn.us/forestry/anniversary.)p.8.
5 *Ibid.*
6 *Ibid.*
7 *Ibid*, page 12.
8 https://en.wikipedia.org.wiki/Slash_(logging), accessed 11-25-2017.
9 Elizabeth Bachmann, "A History of Forestry in Minnesota," 1965. (files.dnr.state.mn.us/forestry/anniversary.),p.12.
10 *Ibid.*, page 13.
11 *Ibid.*

General Andrews was very proud of his part in the establishment of Minnesota's forests, but his services in the cause of forestry were under-appreciated. As Elizabeth Bachman observed, "His generation looked upon forests as superfluous timber which had to be cut down. As he predicted the magnificent pine forests of Minnesota had largely disappeared by the time of his death in 1922, and lumber was being imported from the Pacific Coast states.[12]

A railway fire protection inspector was appointed in 1912: William M. Byrne. That same year an amendment to the 1911 law required railway companies to take more precautions with their ash pan and spark arresting devices on locomotives than had previously been the case. William Byrne pioneered in establishing locomotive inspection as well as an elaborate system of patrolling after trains during dry periods. He developed the laws covering the design and maintenance of spark arresting devices, inspecting of locomotives, devising the system of railroad patrols, making certain that rights of ways were kept clear of combustible material, and checking on fires of railroad origin. He is credited with making the system efficient and self-operating.[13] However, as Francis Carroll states, "Even with proper equipment the old coal-burning locomotives dropped embers from their fire boxes and blew sparks from their smoke stacks, thus starting fires."[14]

In 1913 the Legislature enacted a number of laws relating to forests and fires, some of the most notable being those related to the strengthening of extant laws about the safe disposal of logging slash. The following year saw the first extensive tree planting work undertaken, unfortunately to minimal success.[15] But steps were slowly being made in the right direction.

Average weather conditions greatly assisted vastly underfunded and undermanned fire prevention efforts until the drought years of 1917 and 1918. To make matters worse, many of the experienced fire fighters were away on the battle fronts of World War I. Even railroad working crews were in short supply. Other circumstances contributed to the dangerous conditions. To cite a few examples, peat bogs and swamp lands had been drained, land cleared, and careless but urgent war-time logging had left a tremendous fire hazard in the forested areas of Minnesota. In 1917 alone a million acres burned.[16] The stage was set for another disastrous conflagration.

On October 12, 1918, many of the small fires that had been burning throughout the forest area during the terribly hot and dry summer and fall erupted into at least five or six major blazes. The towns of Cloquet and Moose Lake, as well as many smaller villages and settlements, were almost wiped off the map. (Included in the tally of areas either partially or completely burned besides Cloquet and Moose Lake were Kettle River, Lawler, Adolph, Munger, Five Corners, Harney, Grand Lake, Maple Grove, Twig, Barnum, Matthew, Atkinson, French River, Clifton, Brookston, Brevator, Pike Lake, Pine Hill, Kalevala, Salo, Split Rock, Automba, McGregor, and Warba.) The entire city of Duluth was seriously threatened for a time by this catastrophe that took about 453 lives.[17] (See Addendum B for information about the Fires and Duluth itself.)

The fires in and near Hermantown appeared to have had two sources. The first was the main Cloquet Fire that began along the Great Northern Railway tracks west of Brookston on the south bank of the St. Louis River at milepost 62 and 67. (Railroads have mile markers, called 'mile posts.' A mile post' is the geographical measure of a railroad line. Mile posts allow train crews to determine their exact location along otherwise nondescript stretches of geography.)[18] The second, which merged with parts of the Cloquet Fire, consisted of fires started near Alborn along the tracks of the Duluth Missabe and Northern railroad, and swept east and south into the outskirts of Duluth.[19]

---

12 *Ibid.*, p. 13.

13 *Ibid..*, p. 14.

14 Frances M. Carroll, Crossroads in Time: A History of Carlton County Minnesota, Carlton County Historical Society, Cloquet, Minnesota, 1987, p. 222.

15 Elizabeth Bachmann, "A History of Forestry in Minnesota," 1965. (files.dnr.state.mn.us/forestry/anniversary.), p. 15.

16 *Ibid.*, p. 16.

17 *Ibid.*

18 Carpenter, Richard. "Railroad Signals of the US: Mileposts and Whistle-stops," http://www.railroadsignals.us/support/mileposts/index.htm. Accessed 11-25-2017.

19 Francis M .Carroll and Franklin R. Raiter, "The People Versus the Government: The 1918 Cloquet Fire and the Struggle for Compensation," Journal *of*

After every major fire the Minnesota Legislature assayed to enact laws to prevent and minimize forest fire death and destruction, and the Fires of 1918 were no exception. In another desperately dry year - 1919 - an important forestry law was enacted by the Legislature: a burning permit law.[20] This law specified the time of starting and the conditions under which open fires would be permitted in certain parts of the state. It also provided for the issuance of permits to start fires in certain cases. Up until that time, a person could start a fire wherever and whenever, regardless of the fire danger.

*Forest History*, Vol 29, No. 1 (Jan., 1985), page 4. Published by Oxford University Press on behalf of Forest History Society and American Stable URL http://www.jstor.org/stable/4004968. Accessed: 9-12-2017.

20 *Ibid.*, p. 19.

# Chapter Two: Wildfires

A wildfire has been defined as ". . . an uncontrolled fire that is wiping out large areas of land. It is typically fires . . . that went unnoticed and got out of hand. These fires sometimes burn for days and weeks. They can wipe out an entire forest and destroy almost every organic matter in it."[21] Other names for wildfires are forest fires, peat fires, grass fires, and brush fires, depending upon the type of vegetation being burnt. Most often a variety of materials are being incinerated.

Wildfires are usually grouped into five general types. A ground wildfire is the first type. It burns organic material in the soil, usually under vegetation or forest litter. This type of wildfire is slower burning, and burns by glowing combustion.

The second type is the surface wildfire that burns on the surface of the ground, incinerating materials such as dry leaves, as well as broken twigs and branches on the forest floor. As opposed to ground wildfires, surface wildfires spread quickly.

Crown fires, the third type of wildfires, burn from tree top to tree top, and spread very quickly with huge flames and intense heat.

The fourth type of wildfire is a spot-fire, and is terrifying. Sometimes winds blow fireballs from burning treetops to other spots, starting new wildfires apart from the main blaze. These fireballs are most commonly called firebrands.

A conflagration is the fifth type. This type is a large wildfire, usually enhanced with wind action and firebrands. It spreads aggressively.[22]

Author Stephen J. Pyne adds another type of wildfire: a mass fire. After observations and studies of huge and destructive wildfires in the western U. S., he wrote a book titled, *Fire in America,* documenting his research. He wrote, ". . . a mass fire that remains stationary is a *firestorm;* one that moves is a *conflagration.*" [23]Fortunately, mass fires are not common. Mass fires could have been ground, surface, and crown wildfires initially, before maturing into a mass fire. Unlike ordinary wildfires, mass fires are typically born when two or more smaller wildfires suddenly merge into a single eruption of flame. Often this is a main fire and spot fires that have been spawned by firebrands exploding from the main fire. The single combination of flames may be as high as one hundred feet over the tops of the trees, or two hundred feet above the ground. They advance as fast as 15 miles per hour on level ground, and much faster on a slope. The mass fire creates huge convection columns that tower over the surrounding countryside, radiating heat downward and drying out the fuel in their paths.

Mass fires often generate enormous winds, often of hurricane velocity. These winds sometimes begin to rotate and act like tornadoes of fire that may advance well ahead of the main mass fire front. Because of the robust updraft in their convective columns, mass fires typically pick up thousands of flaming or glowing firebrands, some as large as burning logs. These can be carried as much as 18,000 feet into the sky before being thrown miles ahead of the fire fronts, spawning spot fires wherever the firebrands land.

Because mass fires consume their fuel so rapidly, they often exhaust all the available oxygen in the air before they have finished burning all the carbon and volatile gases that have been released from their fuel sources. Vast clouds of black smoke result from this type of fire, carrying a heavy load of unburned carbon. As this superheated black smoke rises, it eventually meets enough oxygen to allow combustion to resume, resulting in sheets of flame across the sky. People on the ground often describe this horrifying condition as the sky being on fire. But an even more terrifying phenomenon can occur. Glowing bubbles of gases released by the fire, which may be as large as a car, may float some

---

21 http://eschooltoday.com/natural-disasters/wildfires/information-on-wildfires.html.
22 *Ibid.*
23 Daniel James Brown, A Flaming Sky:The Great Hinckley Firestorm of 1894, The Lyons Press, 2006, p. 63.

distance ahead of the fire like huge balloons bouncing across the sky before suddenly bursting into flames over the heads of terrified onlookers.[24]

In the fall of 1918 some people in Northeastern Minnesota noticed what was described as a ". . . sickening stench coming from the swamps" that was the telltale odor from the natural creation of highly volatile methane gas.[25] Axe men in Cloquet spoke about how the entire floor of the forest was glowing like an open barbecue pit. The rich black soil of the woods, now as hard as wood, had become converted into a fuel that burned with intense heat. To the depth of a foot, the woodlands around Brookston and Moose Lake were a bed of glowing embers. Every time a breeze stirred, the woods glowed in an angry red shade. All it needed was a wind to send it on the rampage. Few realized that in such an event, the methane gas could provide an explosive catalyst." [26]

Late in the afternoon of October 12, 1918, Cloquet residents heard ". . . a rumble, almost like an approaching thundershower, and the hurricane winds unleashed a red dragon from the woodlands where the methane gas had been imprisoned underground. The igniting gas produced a violent explosion." [27]

When two large fires near each other, they compete over the available fuel and oxygen in the area between them. Both fires generate tremendous winds, but the area between them may be relatively still as the countervailing winds tend to neutralize each other. The fires both radiate heat down onto the surface, with the land between the two fires growing extremely hot. Instantaneously one of the fires pulls the other one into itself and the fires literally blow up. The area between the two fires, having been heated and dried by both, is incinerated in a matter of moments. The mass fire that results is likely to be far larger and more dangerous than the two wildfires that spawned it.[28]

The result of a mass wildfire is devastation. The soil itself can be virtually destroyed. Wildfires are capable of raising the temperatures of forest soils to over 900 degrees C., which wipes away almost all the organic value of the soil itself. The watershed can also be impacted. Burned organic matter in the soil affects the natural layering of the soils, hindering infiltration and percolation. This makes the soil surfaces rain water repellent. The net result is that rain water is unable to drain into the water tables, and the run-off on the surface causes erosion. Wildlife is also affected. Although many animals are able to escape or move away from the fires, some young animals and birds do perish.[29]

The part of the 1918 Fires that burned much of Hermantown probably originated at milepost 62. Milepost 62, located west just outside of Brookston, was a 2,000 foot long siding called "O'Brien's Spur" where large amounts of lumber, cordwood, telephone poles and the like were loaded. A small fire broke out on October 10$^{th}$ in the grass and materials beside the tracks after the passage of a Great Northern local passenger train. For the next two days neighbors and train crews put out the small blazes, but with the dry conditions the fire crept into the wood chips and bark, and from there spread onto the piles of lumber and other wood piled in the area.[30]

As Daniel James Brown states, "The fires entered the outskirts of Duluth when four-to-six hundred carloads of lumber ignited more or less simultaneously, resulting in an explosion of flames much like the one that had occurred in Hinckley in 1894 when the lumberyards there had gone up in flames."[31]

H. W. Richardson, weatherman at the U. S. Weather Bureau at Duluth, wrote extensively about the 1918 Fire

24 *Ibid.*, p. 64.
25 Frances X. Sculley, *Op.cit.*, pp. 56-57.
26 *Ibid., p. 57.*
27 *Ibid.*, p. 58.
28 *Ibid.*, p. 65.
29 http://eschooltoday.com/natural-disasters/wildfires/information-on-wildfires.html
30 Carroll, Francis M. "The Cloquet Fire,", *Crossroads in Time; A History of Carlton County, Minnesota,* p. 230, published by the Carlton County Historical Society, 1987.
31 Brown, Daniel James. *Under a Flaming Sky: The Great Hinckley Firestorm of 1894,* 2006, pp. 196-197.

in *The Geographical Review* of April, 1919. He noted the extreme character of the Fire, which he emphasized, was ". . . not merely one great fire, but fifty to seventy-five or more which united to a considerable extent. . . The wind," he stated, ". . . fanned the fires to huge proportions, and then, with the increasing energy developed by the consequent violent air movement attending rapid combustion on such an enormous scale, advanced over vast areas with almost incredible speed." [32]

As predisposing factors, Richardson observed that for some days before the fires there had been numerous brush and peat-bog fires simmering over limited areas. Many of the peat lands had been previously been drained. Fire in peat is difficult to extinguish, J. R. Lloyd of the Chicago Weather Bureau noted, and he suggested that the smoldering peat bogs became a major source of the 1918 Forest Fires. Peat fires have been observed to burn from one summer to another, even under a heavy covering of snow during the intervening winter. These fires smoldered for months until the conditions of October 12$^{th}$ combined to make them explode.[33] They were traceable to various causes, he continued, such as the carelessness of campers, automobiles, train crews, and on the part of farmers who burned brush to clear the land. It being quite common to see small fires in the autumn of the year, he said, the public all too often didn't pay much attention to them. Even though the drought was severe, and the summer and fall had been the driest for 48 years, little heed was given to handling fire with requisite care. [34]

Fires can be very capricious by nature, as Richardson said. "On one side of a road there would be nothing but a charred tangle of fallen or partly fallen tree trunks, or a mass of ashes extending for miles with here and there a stump or boulder showing, while on the opposite side for the distance of a mile or more trees and shrubbery and grass would be untouched. A house and barn would be burned to ashes while between the two might stand an undamaged haystack. Occasionally houses were left intact while all around would be desolation; or perhaps one small area of forest might be left inviolate while for miles in all directions nothing but burned waste could be seen." [35]

Richardson opined about the possible reasons why the 1918 Fires were so devastating. He laid the blame on an inadequate forest ranger service; over-drainage of swamp lands and lack of control gates for drainage ditches; lack of supervision and control of land-clearing as well as of logging operations, especially over the burning of brush; insufficient forestry laws and ability to enforce the existing laws; inability to punish offenders; public ignorance of or indifference to forestry laws already enacted; and the inability to quickly warn people living in then isolated sections such as Northeastern Minnesota.[36]

Seven years after the 1918 Fires, another complex of fires occurred in Minnesota, Wisconsin, and Michigan, burning 1.4 million acres. By that time, there was little left to burn in the Upper Midwest. The virgin pine forest that had covered the region less than one hundred years before was irretrievably gone, lost through logging or fires. Even the land left behind was burned, with organic materials that had accumulated and enriched the soil over eons being incinerated. In some places this organic material was twelve feet thick. The gravelly soil, sand, and rock that remained would never again support a white pine forest of the scope the first pioneers saw as virtually inexhaustible.[37]

---

32 Richardson, H. W. "The Northeastern Minnesota Forest Fires of October 12, 1918," *Geographical Review,*_Vol. 7, No. 4 (Apr., 1919), p. 221.

33 Lloyd, J. R. "The Forest Fire-Weather Service in the Lake States," *Monthly Weather Review,* January, 1931, The Weather Bureau, Chicago, IL. https://docs.lib.noaa.gov/rescue/mwr.059-mwr.

34 Richardson, Op cit., p. 221.

35 Richardson, Op.cit., p. 228.

36 *Ibid.*, p. 231.

37 *Ibid.*

# Chapter Three: A Disastrous Year

It is difficult to imagine a more wretched time for humanity than the fall of 1918. The Great War, World War I—the so-called "war to end all wars" –was grinding to a furious conclusion, leaving almost 9 million combatants dead in its wake and millions more who would succumb to malnutrition and disease in a ruined Europe. The U.S. Army was leading the fighting and suffering heavy casualties. Hometown newspapers across Minnesota and the nation, which had pictured handsome young men heading off to war in France in 1917, were using the same photos with stories of violent deaths in places such as St. Mihiel and Belleau Wood. [38]

On its heels, an influenza outbreak—the Spanish flu, as it was commonly known—was ramping up. The grim tally of the dead from this pandemic would make even the staggering number of casualties of World War I seem trivial by comparison. Five hundred million people were infected, and between fifty and one hundred million died worldwide.[39]Although statistics were not kept at the local level, more than 10,000 Minnesotans perished from the Spanish Flu, with the national death toll at about 675,000 according to the US Department of Health and Human Services. [40] Influenza arrived in northeastern Minnesota during the week following the Fires, hitting hard and spreading quickly. As Tim Brady noted in an article titled "Fire and Flu" in the magazine *Minnesota Medicine*, "With just 29 physicians and 15 nurses to serve the region, getting to every desperately ill patient in such a vast district was an impossibility." [41] Almost all of the available medical students had been drafted into military service, exacerbating the situation. [42] By the time the Armistice had been signed the following month, six doctors finally arrived in Duluth from Chicago to help the sick. But by then, the first wave of influenza had peaked, despite the fact that it would wax and wane in Minnesota throughout the winter of 1918 and 1919 and return slightly altered but still deadly in 1920.[43] People from the Township of Herman did not escape the Spanish Flu.

The people of many areas of Northeastern Minnesota had to suffer yet another tragedy: horrific wildfires. Scarcely could they know that on October 12, 1918, a cataclysm of apocalyptic destruction would strike them at home, literally wiping people, livestock, farms, and buildings—including three of the Hermantown Schools—from the face of the earth.

Although often referred to as "The 1918 Forest Fire," as well as the "Cloquet-Moose Lake Fire," it was not one fire but five or six major fires that burned generally from west to east on October 12th. One later analysis showed a possibility of a total of between 50 and 75 smaller fires. [44]

Late in the afternoon of October 10th, farmers northwest of Cloquet noticed smoke rising alongside tracks of the Great Northern Railroad where sparks from a departing train had ignited the dry brush. People rushed to extinguish the flames, but a combination of parched autumnal conditions, an abundance of wood products stacked along the siding, and persistent winds combined to eventually whip the blaze into a massive inferno that began a rapid and inexorable advance to the south and east.[45] Even though the area had been extremely dry since 1916, logging companies still burned piles of branches to clean up their operations, and smoke from burn piles was a common sight. But it must have been unusually dense on October 10th, when the Duluth Weather Bureau report described the thick smoke

38 Tim Brady, "Feature: Fire and Flu. A Fire in Northeastern Minnesota at the Height of the 1918 Flu Pandemic Tested the State's Disaster-Response Mettle, January 2005. http://minnesotamedicine.com/Past-Issues, Accessed 10-15-2014.

39 "1918 Flu Pandemic," https:enWikipedia/org/wiki/1918_flu_pandemic.

40 Davis Helberg., ed, et. al, "1918: Fire, Flu and War," *Esko's Corner: An Illustrated History of Esko and Thomson Township*, X-Presso Books, 2013, page 166.

41 *Ibid.*

42 *Ibid.*

43 *Ibid.*

44 Davis Helberg, ed., chapter by C. Philip Johnson, "The 1918 Fire," *Esko's Corner: An Illustrated History of Esko and Thomson Township*, page 157.

45 Frances M. Carroll and Franklin Roy Raiter, "Milepost 62 and the Fires in Brookston and Fond du Lac," *The Fires of Autumn: The Cloquet-Moose Lake Disaster of 1918,* St. Paul; Minnesota Historical Press, 1990, p. 25-27, 38-39.

over Lake Superior from the smoldering fires scattered over the area. [46] Two days later, on October 12th, the fire blew up and overran Hermantown.

"In the afternoon there was all kinds of smoke, and then we heard roaring just like thunder." So begins the testimony of Anna Hanson of Solway as described in *The Fires of Autumn,* by Francis M. Carroll and Franklin Roy Raiter. The authors' accounting of the Hanson family's harrowing ordeal provides a glimpse into the panic and epic destruction that also prevailed throughout Hermantown that day:

"We thought it was thunder when it was roaring like that, but when we looked out we saw the flames in the treetops," Anna Hanson remembered. A little after 5 PM she and her husband . . . and their five children got into their Ford automobile. With the fourteen-year-old son driving, they attempted to flee to Duluth by way of the Seville Road and the Miller Trunk Line. At about 5:30, just past the Jackson School, the Ford was engulfed in flames and they ran into the ditch. They abandoned the burning automobile and attempted to make their way back about three blocks to the school. "There was fire all around us. It was raining on us—fire raining on us. When we went to the Jackson School it was [fire] storming and knocked the children down in the road." They stayed outside while the buildings around were burning, but after the fire subsided they went into the Jackson School and stayed there until about 2 A.M., when the Minnesota Home Guard came and took them to Duluth. (The Minnesota Home Guard was created by the state to handle necessary duties within the state. This was especially necessary at the time because many of the state's National Guard units had been called to active duty during World War I. Included in its organization was a Motor Corps Battalion.) [47] [48]

That the Jackson School itself did not burn was nothing short of a miracle, especially in light of the fact that the old, one-room Jackson Schoolhouse—repurposed as a clubhouse for the Jackson Farmer's Club and located on the same property—was destroyed. It was a miracle repeated at both Garfield and the new Washington School in the hub of the community where neighboring St. Paul's German Church did burn. "There were few buildings left in the Town," Art Fichtner writes, "but the school district came out very well with all three of the comparatively new two-room schools and the old one-room Garfield School escaping the fire." Fichtner is only 75 correct in his assessment. The two-room Lincoln School in Adolph was consumed by fire along with the other two western schools, Roosevelt and McKinley.[49] Nevertheless, the fact that the three eastern schoolhouses came through the firestorm relatively unscathed was a sliver of solace during the darkest period in local history. "Fourteen of our citizens were found dead in Hermantown," Art Fichtner reports, "But a considerable number who died as a direct result of the fire but survived long enough to be taken to Duluth hospitals were not recorded in our town records." [50] The shock of this ordeal was felt throughout the region: 1500 square miles burned, 453 lives lost, 52,000 people injured or displaced, 38 communities destroyed, and an estimated $7.3 million in property damage.[51]

As the smoke cleared and the ashes settled, the residents of Hermantown took stock. *The Fires of Autumn* describes the post-apocalyptic landscape they faced: "The settlement in Hermantown was badly damaged. Almost every farm in the township was partially burned. This was prosperous dairy farming country, with herds as large as fifty head. Much of the livestock was killed, and those that survived could not be fed, because most haystacks burned." [52]

With so many of their homes, their livelihoods, their neighbors, and half their schools gone, it would be a long, bleak winter for the survivors in Hermantown.

---

46 Davis Helberg, ed.,chapter by C. Philip Johnson, *Op. cit.,* page 156.

47 Tim Brady, "Feature: Fire and Flu; a Fire in Northeastern Minnesota at the Height of the 1918 Flu Pandemic Tested the State's Disaster-Response Mettle," *Minnesota Medicine.* http://minnesotamedicine.com/Past-Issues, January, 2005.

48 Frances M. Carroll and Franklin Roy Raiter, "The Fires Above Duluth," *Op.cit.,* pp. 67-68.

49 The October 15, 1918 edition of the *Duluth News Tribune* reported: "Not a house remains in Adolph. Every house in the little village, the new schoolhouse, and farm buildings west of the village were wiped out.

50 Arthur Fichtner, *Op.cit.,* p. 7.

51 Lois E. Johnson, "Commemorating the 80th Anniversary of the Fires of 1918," *The Minnesota History Interpreter,* Vol. XXVI, No. 6, June 1998.

52 Frances M. Carroll and Franklin Roy Raiter, Op.cit., p. 69.

# Chapter Four: Unique Weather Conditions

Most written memoirs of the Fire's survivors recount what a dry year or two had preceded the 1918 Fires. Their memories appear to be corroborated by a Duluth meteorologist of the era as well as a meteorologist and a fire control scientist five decades later.

The person in charge of the U. S. Weather Bureau at Duluth, H. W. Richardson, wrote a comprehensive article in 1919 for a magazine called *Geographical Review.* His article summarizes the Fires and reports on their scope for his readers who may have been unfamiliar with the 1918 Fires. As he begins his meteorological section, he wrote, "The conditions which favored the full development of the great fires were primarily those of drought (the season being the driest for 48 years) and the fresh winds that occurred on October 12." [53]

The morning of October 12, 1918, dawned in a fairly typical manner for the season, with the exception of the continuation of the exceptionally dry weather. As he explained, ". . . the air-pressure gradient was by no means extraordinary. Fair weather and winds from westerly directions, fresh or moderately strong (about 30-miles an hour rates), were indicated, and in addition a 'small craft' wind warning was ordered displayed on western Lake Superior at 10:30 A.M." [54] Nothing appeared to be really out of the ordinary at the Duluth Weather Bureau until about 12:30 P.M., when smoke began moving in from the west.

However, the smoke was increasing steadily, until about 2:30 P.M. when it increased to the point where the sun appeared red, and became obscured most of the time. Mr. Richardson noted that the hiding of the sun was an alarming sight, since it was common to fires of unusual character. The wind by this time was gradually increasing also, reaching 30 to 40 miles per hour rates from the west at times until about 3 P.M., after which there was a steady rise to 50 to 60 miles per hour rates from the west-southwest-northwest between 4:15 P.M. and 9 P.M. Between 9 P.M. and 2 A.M. the wind continued at speeds of 40 miles per hour, after which time it died down considerably. Officially, at the weather bureau station located midway up the Hillside of Duluth, the highest five minute rate was 65 miles an hour from the west at 5:52 P.M., while the highest wind gust for a shorter period of time was 76 miles an hour about that same time.[55]

Between 4 and 5 P.M. dense smoke drifted rapidly in from the west, indicating ". . .that fires of marked intensity and extent were occurring in the vicinity." [56] In Duluth by 4:30 P.M. the city lights had to be turned on, due to the smoke induced darkness. [57]Occasionally during the late afternoon and into the night the dense smoke showed a deep red color from the south to north, Richard continues to state that it wasn't until about 5:30 P.M. that Duluthians began to realize the danger, when authentic news of the disaster in adjoining districts began reaching the city. Brookston, a town 35 miles west of Duluth, was belatedly reported to be destroyed by Fire at 4 P.M. News was only able to be relayed over telephone and telegraph lines from the southwest, west, and northwest, until about 6 P.M., when most lines were either destroyed or severely damaged.[58]

H. W. Richardson of the U.S. Weather Bureau at Duluth described the extent of the Fires. Near Duluth, from west to north and including the northern suburbs there was an irregular frontage of 10 miles, while at Cloquet the front was from 6 to 8 miles, and about 7 miles at Moose Lake. However, as he noted, "Occasionally vast billows of detached flames would

---

53 H.W. Richardson, "The Northeastern Minnesota Forest Fires of October 12, 1918," *Geographical Review*, vol. no. 4 (April, 1919), page 221. *JSTOR, JSTOR*, www.jstor.org/stable/207371.

54 *Ibid.*, page 221.

55 *Ibid.*, page 223.

56 *Ibid.*, page 223.

57 Herbert Lyman, "Smoke from Minnesota Forest Fires," "*Monthly Weather Review*, November, 1918, Weather Bureau, Washington. https://cods.lib.noaa.gov.resue/mwr/046/mwr-046-11-0506.page 506.

58 *Ibid.*, page 225.

leap across rivers, streams, small lakes, roads, and other open spaces in front of the walls of fire."[59]

After reviewing synoptic maps of the day, Meteorologist Richardson deduced that the major force of the gale force winds that existed during the late afternoon and night of October 12th were fire created. As he wrote, ". . . the weather map on the morning of that [day] apparently favored wind velocities not much in excess of 30-mile rates. But, inasmuch as numerous small fires were then prevailing over extensive but more or less separated areas, and as the record-breaking drought had caused a tinder-dry condition of vegetation, a wind of any sustained force was all that was required to put into activity a series of united conflagrations that gathered tremendous impetus and quickly thwarted the most desperate attempts at effective control. . .there was an accompanying air movement or combustive draft of hurricane force; that the wind velocity was immeasurably greater . . .and must surely have been blowing at a rate of 80 to 90 miles adjoining the fire fronts from two to six miles or more distant from the station. There was an attendant deafening roar of fire and wind combined."[60]

National notice was given to the smoke cloud as it quickly spread over a large part of the U. S. east of the Missouri River. The speed which the smoke traveled was very notable and unusual. By the next morning, the smoke cloud had spread over the Michigan Peninsula and central Indiana. Twelve hours later strong northwest winds had carried the smoke across Ohio into New York, Pennsylvania, West Virginia, Maryland, and the District of Columbia. By the morning of the 14th the smoke had spread to Charleston, South Carolina and Little Rock, Arkansas.[61] By the evening of October 14th the smoke had reached College Station, Texas, and Thomasville, Georgia, on the east. On October 16th, the smoke cloud covered an area from Valentine, Nebraska, to Portland, Maine, and from the Great Lakes to Little Rock, Arkansas, and Greenville, South Carolina.[62] Not only had the smoke cloud traveled south and east, but also to the west. On October 15th, easterly winds in western Minnesota carried the smoke cloud across most of North Dakota by the 16th, from where it drifted south into Nebraska the following day. [63]

Meteorologist Donald A. Haines and Associate Fire Control Scientist Rodney W. Sando studied conditions leading up to a few great forest fires in the north central region of the U. S., and wrote a detailed report on their findings. One of those fires studied was the October 12, 1918, Fires. As they noted, since the nearby Duluth Weather Bureau was designated a first-order station, it had more complete instrumentation, thus enabling them to reconstruct the weather conditions preceding and during the time of the Fires. [64]

According to their study, the severe drought may well have begun as early as the autumn of 1916, and continued until the October 1918 Fire. The Duluth weather station recorded near all-time low precipitation totals during the pre-fire months. Until that time, Duluth had never experienced a February through September precipitation total less than the 1918 amount of 12.67 inches.

Although the Cloquet observation station received a very light rain totaling only 0.32 of an inch from October 4th through October 8th, it didn't help very much in reducing fire danger, much less relieving the drought. A surprising finding was that the summer of 1918 was cooler than usual, and temperatures averaged quite a bit below normal the month before the Fires. However, ten days before the Fires the temperatures warmed to slightly above normal. Sando and Haines concluded that ". . .if there is a conflagration reaction to temperature, *it is often a short-term response.*" [65]

They also studied soil-water calculations at soil depths of 3 feet, which is the upper rooting depth of grasses. When

59 H.W. Richardson, H.W., *Op.cit., p. 227.*
60 *Ibid.*, pp.230 and 231.
61 Herbert Lyman, *Op.cit.*, p. 506.
62 *Ibid.*, p. 507.
63 *Ibid.*, p. 509.
64 Donald A. Haines and Rodney W. Sando,"Climatic Conditions Preceding Historically Great Fires in the North Central Region," p. 3, published by North Central Forest Experiment Station, 1969. USDA Forest Research PaperNC-34.
65 *Ibid.*,p. 9.

this type of vegetation wilts, they wrote, large amount of fuel become cured and ready to burn. The period in the 1918 Fire season in which vegetation wilted they calculated to be about two months.[66]

Well-above normal sunshine prevailed during every month except May of 1918, they further deduced. Every monthly average through July had a higher percentage of sunshine than would be expected. [67]

Another factor they examined was relative humidity. The average monthly relative humidity was below normal throughout much of the 1918 fire season. As they observed, the ". . . monthly temperature was not abnormally high in . . . the 1918 pre-fire period, but diminished atmospheric moisture seems to have contributed to the explosive fire situation." [68]

Sando and Haines made an apt metaphor to the series of events leading to the fires they studied, including the October 12, 1918, Fires. "A large amount of fuel was usually available before the fire; this would be analogous to a rifle shell. A unique series of climatic events prevailed during much of the fire season—*the shell is loaded into the rifle chamber.* Smaller fires were burning in the forests and bogs—*the hammer is pulled back.* A favorable synoptic weather pattern developed over the region—*the trigger is pulled and the bullet is on its way.*"[69]

The bullet on October 12, 1918, was fatal.

66 *Ibid.*,p. 11.
67 *Ibid.*, p. 12.
68 *Ibid.*, p. 14.
69 *Ibid.*,p. 15.

# Chapter Five: Treating Burn Victims

Even with medical advancements in the 21st century, skin burns are painful and can be deadly. In comparison, medical treatment of burns in 1918 was primitive at best.

A medical textbook from 1909 contained the most up to date information for treating burns of varying degrees of severity. The least severe type of burn, a first degree burn, was treated by smearing the surface of the burn with a light ointment such as rose water ointment or cow's cream.

A second degree burn, which was more severe, was characterized by blisters, redness, swelling, and tenderness. To treat these burns and relieve pain, one method advocated applying a dressing soaked with oil or spread with ointment to protect the burn surface from air. A second treatment proposed was to cover the burn with strips of rubber tissue or with gauze wet with a normal saline solution. A third method was to treat the burned area with an antiseptic dressing which was either allowed to dry or else kept moist. The fourth plan was to leave the burned area exposed to the air in order to dry it up. Then dusted with powder.

The medical textbook's author, Dr. Milton Foote, favored the first or second treatment methods, specifically an oily dressing of equal parts of linseed oil and lime water, or an oily dressing of boric acid and Vaseline. The ointment was to be spread over the burned area with a spatula, much like buttering a piece of bread.

In third degree burns, the most serious ones, deep structures of skin layers have been destroyed by the heat. The skin appears to be white because blood cannot circulate through the destroyed blood vessels. Eventually the dead skin sloughs off.

Treatment of third degree burns involved draining any pockets of pus as they formed, and then applying a moist antiseptic dressing. The administration of morphine either hypodermically or by mouth during the first 24 hours to relieve the excruciating pain was highly recommended.

Skin material sloughing off was to be cut away as soon as it loosened. In large burned areas the central parts of the skin often loosened before the edges, and in that case incisions were made through the sloughed areas to permit the escape of pus and secretions.

To prevent contractions, plaster bandages and splints were often needed to keep the burned area fully extended during the healing process. Unfortunately, scars were permanent and often very visible.[70] People in the Hermantown area remembered classmates and friends and neighbors with burn scars and who suffered with pain from their deep burns for the rest of their lives.

However, according to the Medical Officer in charge of the Home Guard, many burn victims at the Duluth Armory were treated by the paraffin method of treatment of burns, whereby the parts of their bodies burned were immersed in paraffin wax.[71]

A lot of people did not receive medical care from a doctor. Medical treatment for burns in the late 1800s and early 1900s often consisted of home remedies. These home treatments consisted of treating burns with quite a variety of salves and ointments: black mud, cow dung, raw egg and vinegar, pig fat, boiled beans, beeswax, honey, oak leaves, and powdered silver, to name a few. Most of these treatments did more harm than good, since they introduced new pathogens into the wounds and then sealed them in, creating an especially conducive environment for the growth of anaerobic bacteria like *Clostridium perfringens,* as well as *Streptococcus, E. coli, and Staphylococcus aureus.* Even the

---

70 Edwin Milton Foote, A.M., M.D., *A Text-Book of Minor Surgery*, published by D. Appleton and Company of New York, 1909, pp. 25-29. http://www.archive.org/details/textbookofminors00footuoft

71 Roger M. Weaver, *Major M. Weaver Scrapbook*, "Report from Medical Officer, Captain Arthur H. Collins, Medical Corps, in charge of 3rd Division Minnesota Home Guard to Commanding Officer of Same," Dated October 26, 1918, Northeast Minnesota Historical Center Collections, Archives and Special Collections, Kathryn A. Martin Library, University of Minnesota Duluth.

three least harmful treatments—honey, oak leaves, and powdered silver—were of limited healing assistance except to relatively superficial first degree burns. (Honey has antimicrobial agents and absorbs moisture out of the atmosphere, thus keeping the wound moist. Oak leaves have tannic acid, which is an astringent that essentially 'tans' the skin, in a similar fashion to the manner in which cowhides are tanned to make leather. Silver ions have antiseptic properties that make silver sulfadiazine and silver nitrate among the most useful burn treatments.) The mixture of lime water and linseed oil soothed pain and didn't significantly contaminate the wounds with new bacteria. [72]

Treatment in a hospital at Duluth consisted of cleaning the burns with carbolic acid and dressing them, in layers, with petroleum jelly, old linen, cotton, another layer of linen, and finally, waxed paper or oilcloth held in place by bandages. However, the inevitable consequences of major burns were not addressed by this treatment. Major burns are characterized by a loss of fluid from the bloodstream, edema and its resulting swelling, physical shock from the burn itself, deepening and spreading of wounds, and an overactive metabolism, followed by the development of a massive bacterial and fungal infection under all those layers of linen and waxed paper.

Reportedly, burn wards of the day were notorious for their atmosphere of hopelessness and for the stench of rotting flesh. [73] Daniel Brown leads off his chapter about skin burns with a stark paragraph. He writes, "Being badly burned is just about the worst thing that can happen to a body short of immediate dismemberment and death. No other type of injury creates the same kind of long-lasting physiological mayhem, the same potential for pain, the same degree of uncertainty about the outcome, the same kind of disfigurement for those who manage to survive."[74] _

The physical progression of second degree or higher burns that cover more than 20 percent of the body's surface area is gruesome. Edema results in severe swelling of the lips, genitals, throat and mouth in particular. What's worse, the swelling tissues press on blood vessels and internal organs. Swollen linings of the airway threaten to close off the flow of air to the lungs, making breathing even more difficult than it already was from the smoke in the air.

The bloodstream loses the proteins, fats, sugars, and electrolytes that it normally carries, including necessary elements like potassium and magnesium that regulate the function of the muscles and various vital organs. Blood gradually thickens into a kind of sludge that the heart struggles to pump around the body. Lungs fill with fluid; blood pressure drops suddenly, as does body temperature. Patients shiver uncontrollably, even in a warm environment. Then burn shock sets in. The pulse grows weak and erratic; fingertips and other extremities turn blue; individual cells begin to die; tissue is damaged, and organs may fail. The burn victim becomes lethargic and unresponsive, and often dies at this point. [75]

All of this occurs during the initial twenty-four hours of being burned. But then things often got worse, if the burn victim was still alive. As was noted by an author trained in burn care, ". . . a burn is an evolving wound; the initial injury is only the beginning of an ongoing disease process that must be stopped or it will end in death." The body is overwhelmed by the magnitude of the damage of the burns, and in an attempt to heal itself can make things worse. The burns may expand over time, deprived of oxygen under the dead tissue. They also may work deeper into the underlying tissue and spread outward, acting as scavenger cells destroying both dead cells as well as adjacent living cells. [76]

Also on the second day after the initial burn injury the body may begin to cannibalize itself, a condition called hyper-metabolism. To fight the burn injury, the body needs enormous amounts of fuel and oxygen. The metabolic system responds to these needs and burns calories at a furious rate. However, it doesn't burn fat as it ordinarily would, but instead consumes protein, making the victim waste away. As the body's lean mass diminishes, so does its ability to fight infections. Even from the moment the flames subside, masses of microbial life begin to attack the

72 Daniel James Brown, *Under a Flaming Sky: The Great Hinckley Firestorm of 1894*, pp. 171-173.
73 *Ibid.*, p. 173.
74 *Ibid.*, p. 131.
75 *Ibid.*, pp. 131-134.
76 Barbara Ravage, "A Riot in the Body," *Burn Unit: Savings Lives After the Flames, pp. 43-46. Da Capo Press, 2004.*

burn victim from both inside and outside his body. A serious burn injury breaks the protective seal of skin, and allows bacteria to enter and move downward through the burn itself and enter the bloodstream. Yeast infections often follow, making things worse. The result can be sepsis, organ failure, and death.

Some people were of the opinion that it was better to be made unconscious by the lack of oxygen first before being actually consumed by flames.[77] By the end of the 20th century new life-saving therapies for burn victims were discovered, and burns that had carried a near 100 percent mortality rate at the beginning of the century carried rates as low as 5 percent.[78]

77 *Ibid.*
78 Daniel James Brown, *Op.cit.*, p. 134.

# Chapter Six: Finding Refuge

The Fires burned over a large area, as a local newspaper article emphasized six days later. "Within easy driving distance of Third Avenue West and Superior Street, just back over the hills that overlook the harbor is one blackened area of fully 400 square miles in which buildings are scarce and ruins are prolific. . . . From Pike Lake to Five Corners, Twig, and all through the Hermantown, Munger, and Adolph country the story goes just the same. It tells its own tale of need."[79] Areas around Grand Rapids, Aitkin, northward toward Virginia, and as far south as halfway between Moose Lake and Hinkley were still threatened by fire. Although the fire survivors fled to these areas immediately outside of the fire danger zone, they were by no means completely assured of being safe from new fires. They had to remain vigilant and ready to flee any new fires that might suddenly erupt.

With such a large area being virtually consumed by flames, where to house the fire survivors became a pressing concern. Help was officially offered almost immediately. Duluth's mayor, C. R. Magney, was quoted as saying on the night of October 12$^{th}$, "Duluth will care not only for her own but for the homeless and stricken from other cities. We are all going to do the best for them." [80] Superior Wisconsin's mayor, F. A. Baxter, also voiced a similar message the same night. In it he called upon the people of Superior to volunteer food and lodging to the forest fire refugees who were brought there. He pointed out that they would need breakfast, and urged everyone who could care for anybody to call the Commercial Club. As his official statement said, "Refugees have been brought into Superior from the fire districts. It is probable that 5,000 are here. These people are being cared for in clubs and halls. It is necessary for the people of Superior to take them into their homes. We must start feeding them this morning. I, therefore, call upon the people of Superior to meet the situation by throwing open their homes to these unfortunates, at least for meals. Headquarters have been established at the Commercial club. Will you call there and leave word as to when and how many you can care for?"[81]

Many people who had relatives in the unburned areas of Duluth sought safety and comfort with family there. Those who did not have relatives or friends to whom they could turn were temporarily lodged in various facilities. Newspaper articles in the Duluth News Tribune in the days after the conflagration noted the names of many fire refugees and where they were temporarily located. Pages of alphabetized listings, by surname, were given of those who were looking for family members. The title of one such article aptly summarized the situation: "Refugees Registered in Duluth, Read Them and Help Reunite Fire Stricken Families." The lengthy lists give the names of the people along with their known address, under the location in which they were temporarily lodged. The first listing was the Duluth Armory; then the St. Louis Hotel; Central Y.M.C.A.; Holland Hotel; McKay Hotel; Lenox Hotel; Masonic Temple; St. Mary's Hospital; St. Luke's Hospital; Boy's Y.M.C.A.; Davidson Home; Spalding Hotel; and, the Shriners. Single women were taken to the Y. W. C. A. Injured persons were rushed late in the night to St. Mary's and St. Luke's Hospitals as well as the Duluth Armory, by autos from Duluth and Superior as well as an ore dock ambulance.[82] The Masonic Temple Building on Lake Avenue sheltered 66 refugees from Cloquet, with cots set up in the basement for sleeping and food supplied by the Red Cross.[83] Residents close to Proctor were taken to the Proctor High School and the Duluth Missabe and Northern (DM&N) Railroad machine shops

---

79 "Losses Close to Duluth Appall; Settlers, Farmers Rally After First Shock, Begin Digging Spuds, "*Duluth News Tribune*, October 18, 1918. Online at GenealogyBank.com. http://www.genealogybank.com/gbnk.newspapers/doc.

80 "Arms of Duluth Open to Victims; First Aid Given. Army Thronged with Patients Cared for by Red Cross Women-Heroic Rescues," *Duluth News Tribune*, October 13, 1918. Online at GenealogyBank.com. http://www.genealogybank.com/doc.newspapers/image.

81 "Mayor Baxter Calls on Superior to Aid Refugees, "*Duluth News Tribune*, October 13, 1918. Online at GenealogyBank.com. http://www.genealogybank.com/doc/newspapers/image.

82 "Arms of Duluth Open to Victims; First Aid Given," *Duluth News Tribune*, October 13, 1918. Online at GenealogyBank.com. http://www.genealogybank.com/doc/newspapers/image.

83 "Refugees Registered in Duluth, Read Them and Help Reunite Fire Stricken Familes," *Duluth News Tribune*, October 14, 1918, Online at GenealogyBank.com. http://www.genealogybank.com/doc/newspapers/image.

in the center of the town, an area of Proctor that did not burn.

One can only imagine the mood of the refugees: shock, unspeakable grief; intense anxiety. However, an anecdote related in the book *Burning An Empire* presents another side to the intense emotions. Author Stewart Holbrook reported that on the morning of October 13th a lumberjack came into a Duluth hotel to rest quietly in a chair of the hotel lobby. He had been fighting fire almost all night, was exhausted, as well as being hung-over from liquid libations. All he wanted to do was sleep off his physical exhaustion, as well as his hang-over. Distraught refugee women would not let him sleep, however, and kept asking him questions about what he had seen as he was fighting the fires. He dealt with the questions until one particularly anxious woman asked him if he had seen anybody burned to death on the Miller Trunk Road. At that question the lumberjack sat up, loudly cursed, and yelled at the poor woman, "That road is corduroyed with the dead for miles." Then he went to sleep, left alone after his angry outburst. Holbrook wrote that incident was reported to him by Jess Colburn of Cloquet, an old lumberjack and survivor of the 1918 Fires.[83a]

Homes, public buildings, clubs, stores, hospitals, and the St. Louis County Courthouse in Duluth were used to temporarily care for the burned and homeless. A grainy newspaper photograph presents a poignant view of grim faced children sitting beside cots. The caption states, "Children Refugees at Court House Jury Room Nursery." [84]

Residents offered complete strangers their compassionate care, including a Duluth couple who offered their house free to fire refugees. [85] Another such generous family was the Henry Bridgeman family of Duluth. An appreciative woman named Ida Josephine Watson wrote a letter to the editor of the Duluth News Tribune, commending the Bridgeman family who had sheltered her and her family, as well as four unidentified Hermantown families, in their own home. Ida wrote that the Bridgeman residence was, "filled with people from far and near. Four families from Hermantown were there, besides dozens of others, all being ministered to by the thoughtful attentions of Mr. and Mrs. Bridgeman." [86]

Refugees from Cloquet and the adjoining countryside were housed at private homes in Carlton, as well as its City Hall, jail, and other public buildings.

The city of Superior, Wisconsin was especially accommodating. Over 3,000 refugees lodged with residents, in public halls, schools, public buildings, Crownhart Hall of the Superior Normal School, Superior High School, Sacred Heart School, the Superior Armory, St. Joseph's Orphanage, Hammond Avenue Presbyterian Church, the Finnish Hall, Christ Lutheran Church, and fraternal lodges. [87]

---

83a Stewart H. Holbrook, "The Story of Cloquet," Burning an Empire: The Story of American Forest Fires (New York: The MacMillan Company, 1943), p.36.

84 "Outfitting Homeless to Start Anew: Children Refugees at Court House Jury Room Nursery," caption from photos, *Duluth News Tribune*, October 16, 1918. Online at GenealogyBank.com. http://www.genealogybank.com/doc/gbml/newspapers/doc.

85 "Couple Offers House Free to Refugees of Fire," *Duluth News Tribune*, October 14, 1918. Online at GenealogyBanik.com. http://www.genealogybank.com/doc/newspapers/image.

86 Ida Josephine Watson, "Letter to Editor," *Duluth News Tribune*, November 19, 1918. Online at GenealogyBank.com. http://www.genealogybank.com.doc.newspapers.doc.

87 "Superior Rushes Measures For Refugee Relief," *Duluth News Tribune*, October 15, 1918. Online at GeneaolgyBank.com. http:www.genealogybank.com/doc/newspapers/image

# Chapter Seven: The Rush to Aid

Many organizations and private individuals offered whatever aid they could to the fire victims. Duluth Churches offering assistance of various types included the Duluth Presbyterian Church, the Pilgrim Church, the First Baptist Church, and the Swedish Mission Churches. The Red Cross circle of the Pilgrim Church made children's garments for fire sufferers, as did the Women's Society Red Cross Circle of the First Baptist Church. A committee of the Swedish Mission denominational group worked under the supervision of the Red Cross Central Committee of Duluth, to supply money and clothing. As the Duluth News Tribune noted, this was very fitting, since many of the fire sufferers were Scandinavians, and quite a few were members of the four Mission churches in the fire-swept districts at Adolph, Five Corners, Moose Lake, and one on the Pike Lake Road. The cash and clothing donated were received by the treasurer of the Swedish Mission Church Relief Committee at its location on West Superior Street in Duluth. [88]

A baker in downtown Duluth called the offices of the Duluth News Tribune and offered to donate some of his baked goods. "I have a lot of bread and things baked up here and they're ready for the refugees if you'll just tell me where to send them," he said. He was referred to the Red Cross women working at the Armory, where hundreds of refugees were to be provided for. [89]

Nine Home Guards from Duluth were sent with a Northern Pacific train bound for Carlton County stations, containing a freight car of provisions on the morning of October 13th. The Zinsmaster-Smith company had donated many cartons of bread; the Bridgeman-Russell Company gave cans of milk; and the wholesale grocery houses of Duluth had provided canned meat, condensed milk, and nut margarine.[90]

The Red Cross, having been thoroughly organized to serve in World War I outreach efforts, was very prepared to assume a prominent role in fire relief efforts while combating the influenza outbreak at the same time. As the Duluth News Tribune reported, "Red Cross women, summoned from their homes by an early call, spread throughout the city, gathered at the Armory. They made an effort to get ready a great supply of influenza masks, anticipating need for them in order to prevent further spread of the epidemic under the disordered conditions resulting from the fire." [91]

St. Luke's and St. Mary's Hospitals donated their care to the fire refugees. As the Duluth News Tribune stated, "The hospitals are offering their services thus for humanity's sake alone. They ask nothing from these poor people except that they get well. Some of the wealthier patients are giving money to the hospitals as they leave, realizing that their supplies are being terribly drained by the large number of patients." [92] Individuals and companies alike gave large donations of food to both hospitals. They also sent in sheets, pillow cases, blankets, and pillows, as well as making new supplies of sheets and pillow cases. Businesses donated bolts of muslin for sheets, and others sent in wagonloads of other bedding. Red Cross workers made masks for use in the hospitals, as well as rolling bandages.[93] Local clothing stores made generous donations of blankets, quilts, and clothing, as well as selling anything the refugees needed at wholesale prices.[94]

---

88 "Arms of Duluth Open to Victims; First Aid Given," *Duluth News Tribune*, October 13, 1918. Online at GenealogyBank.com. http://www.genealogybank.com/doc/newspapers/image.

89 "Baker Offers Bread Supply," *Duluth News Tribune*, October 14, 1918. Online at GenealogyBank.com. http://www.genealogybank.com/doc/newspapers/image.

90 "Special Carries Food Supply to Fire Refugees," *Duluth News Tribune*, October 14, 1918. Online at GenealogyBank.com. http://www.genealogybank.com/doc/newspapers/image.

91 "Arms of Duluth Open to Victims. First Aid Given. Armory Thronged with Patients Cared for by Red Cross Women-Heroic Recues," *Duluth News Tribune*, October 13, 1918. Online at GenealogyBank.com. http://www.genealogybank.com/doc/newspapers/image

92 "135 Burned at Hospitals; Doors Opened to Poor. Nurses and Convalescents Turn Efforts to Speedy Relief of Injured Refugees," *Duluth News Tribune*, October 15, 1918. Online at GenealogyBank.com http://www.genealogybank.com/doc/newspapers/image.

93 *Ibid.*

94 "Superior Rushes Measures For Refugee Relief. Temporary Homes Found for Thousands—Men and Women Aid with Money and Work," *Duluth News Tribune*, October 15, 1918. Online at GenealogyBank.com http://www.genealogybank.com/doc/newspapers/image.

The Minnesota Public Safety Commission sent out sixty boxes of whitefish and pike, under the direction of Game Wardens J. E. Kreager and J. C. Green. Each box weighed from 125 to 150 pounds. Boxes of fish that remained after the initial distribution were placed for safe storage at the Booth's Fish Company's cold storage unit, located in Duluth. From there they were offered to all refugees who wanted fish, and several boxes were sent out to different areas where people already had started rebuilding. [95]

In addition to attending to medical conditions, the Red Cross women also extended an empathetic ear to the distraught and shocked survivors. Families, friends, and neighbors had become separated from each other in the thick smoke as they tried to escape. Since telephone wires and poles had been burned, communication by either telephone or telegraph was virtually impossible for at least several days. At the Armory and other places, there were mothers desperately hunting for their children; husbands anxiously looking for their wives and families; and panic-stricken children separated from their parents.

After the worst flames of the Fires had subsided, travel was difficult. Railroad ties and wooden bridges had been burned. Despite traveling obstacles, anybody with a car was recruited to search for and bring fire victims out of the fire area and to safety in the Duluth and Superior areas. As the Duluth News Tribune reported, "Early in the night, practically every automobile in the city of Duluth had been commandeered in the work of rescuing the residents of Pike Lake, the work farm, the poor farm, Woodland, and Lakeside, but the number was nowhere up to the need, and a message was sent to the Superior automobile association. The police heads of both Superior and Duluth notified the drivers that they were unrestricted as to speed limits." [96] A gas station in Duluth filled gas tanks of those driving cars to rescue fire refugees the night of the fires for free. This was the Standard Oil filling station at 10th Avenue East and Superior Street. [97]

The Duluth Armory functioned as the relief location of the Red Cross. In addition to housing refugees and treating the burn victims, the Armory collected clothing, blankets, and other essential needs for distribution to the other agencies and parties providing assistance. All three floors of the Armory were organized to provide various services to the refugees.

The Fire refugees were urged to register at the Armory to enable their anxious relatives to know whether or not they were alive. Additionally, hundreds of telegrams from out-of-town friends and relatives, unable to be delivered, were kept at the Armory for the recipients, in the hope that they were still alive.

The main floor, where the headquarters was established, was kept in order by the strict military discipline of the Home Guard. Major Towne and Captain Paine were in charge of the entire group of workers, orderlies, and relief cars. At the entrance there was a general information desk ". . . with a corps of stenographers furiously typing out the known names of the refugees, homes to which families were taken, injured in what hospitals, and the myriad other necessary data." [98] In the center of the main floor were tables serving as relief and information desks. Here cards were given out to refugees to register and tell what amounts of clothing they needed. The sides of the main floor's large room contained pens with counters of clothing being sorted and distributed by volunteers. At the back of the main floor, in front of the stage, a clothing repair department was located, in which seamstresses mended and made over donated clothes. The clothing repair department was under the direction of Mrs. C. D. Richards.[99]

---

95 "State Sends Supply of Fish Free for Refugees," *Duluth News Tribune,* October 19, 1918. Online at GenealogyBank.com. http://www.genealogybank.com/doc/newspapers/image

96 "Oil Company Gives Gasoline for Red Cross Service Use," *Duluth News Tribune,* October 14, 1918. Online at GenealogyBank.com. http://www.genealogybank.com/doc/newspapers/image.

97 *Ibid.*

98 Katharine B. Spear, "Emergency Work at Armory a Thing of Mercy; Hundreds of Injured Given Attention," *Duluth News Tribune,* October 15, 1918. Online at GenealogyBank.com/doc/newspapers/image. http://www/genealogybank.com/doc/newspapers/image.

99 "Armory Well Organized to Speed Great Relief Task. Innumerable Departments Care for Needs of Afflicted from Burned Cities and Towns," *Duluth News Tribune,* October 15, 1918. Online at GenealogyBank.com. http://www.genealogybank.com/doc/newspapers/image.

The second floor had a balcony corner where donated shoes were being counted, sorted, and paired off. Additionally, there were surgical dressing workrooms, where women were making gauze influenza masks for every worker, soldier and refugee in the Armory, as well as for distribution to the community at large in an attempt to check the influenza epidemic. Women on the second floor also mended donated garments.[100]

The third floor was divided into emergency rooms, a dispensary, a children's clothing area, and a hospital area. If the incoming survivors were badly burned, they were taken to hospital rooms of the Armory's hospital department when both St. Luke's Hospital and St. Mary's Hospital overflowed with victims. Orderlies from the Home Guard were supplied for the hospital rooms and for all parts of the building where they were needed. The Armory's hospital area treated the less badly burned, and prepared the severely injured for transportation to the actual hospitals, despite the fact that the hospital area had trained nurses in charge and young women serving as nurse's aides.[101] The dispensary was under the direction of Mrs. W. Sumner Covey, who worked in cooperation with several doctors and nurses. The emergency room area had Duluth doctors in charge, and drugs and surgical supplies were given out for those needing immediate medical attention. The children's clothing area had women working all day, sorting, stacking, and grouping sizes of clothing. [102] Also on the third floor was an area headed by Mrs. E. A. Silberstein whose duty it was to hand out materials for necessary clothing to the different church circles and other organizations wishing to do sewing outside of the Armory.

The kitchen was serving food in the basement of the Armory. All patients who were able to eat were served hot drinks and food. Directed by Mrs. Charles N. Thorpe, ". . . a corps of women and young girls started work in the early hours of Sunday morning and served food to workers, many of whom had been at the Armory since the first alarms of Saturday night until noon and after the next day, serving food to the Home Guard who stumbled in hungry and tired for a brief rest, only to leave on other relief and firefighting expeditions and aiding the cooks to serve members of the Fourth Infantry who had been fighting fire. Besides these there were the sick and the refugees who were coming in a constant and countless stream to be warmed, clothed, and fed." [103] The article referred to the workers preparing and providing nourishment to the hungry as the "kitchen police". ". . . the words 'kitchen police' will mean a group of fine women who gave unsparingly of energy and the courage of endurance; cooking, carrying dishes, setting tables, clearing tables, serving food over and over again to ever-coming, ever-increasing numbers of hungry mortals, washing dishes, drying them, and putting them away, only to take them out and set the tables for more servings of food. They were the real workers. They kept the machinery of existence going and gave sustenance where it was most needed." [104]

The federal employment bureau, under the leadership of Miss Katherine King, set up temporary headquarters at the Armory to answer inquiries concerning jobs, including jobs for women as well as men.[105] It became necessary to set up an insurance department area, which worked with local insurance offices to assist the refugees who were insured. [106]

The Duluth News Tribune's Thursday morning edition began with a listing of eighteen tables and the departments assigned to each one. They consisted of the following: General Information; Registration Bureau; Incoming Registration; Disposition of Refugees; Refugee Information; Donations to be called for; Volunteer Workers; Adoptions; Cash Donations for Relief fund; Distribution cards; Clothing distribution; Receiving and Sorting station;

---

100 Katharine B. Spear, *Op.cit.*
101"Armory Well Organized to Speed Great Relief Task. Innumerable Departments Care for Needs of Afflicted from Burned Cities and Towns," *Duluth News Tribune*, October 15, 1918. Online at GenealogyBank.com. http://www.genealogybank.com
102 Katharine B. Spear, *Op. cit.*
103 Katharine B. Spear, *Op. cit.*
104 *Ibid.*
105 "Strict Discipline Obtains at Armory [sic.]; Beehive hums. Clean Bedding Needed; Refugees Must Register; Cloquet Sends Call for Clothing," Duluth *News Tribune*, October 15, 1918. Online at GenealogyBank.com. http://www.genealogybank.com/gbnk/newspapers/doc.
106"Armory Well Organized to Speed Great Relief Task. Innumerable Departments Care for Needs of Afflicted from Burned Cities and Towns," *Duluth News Tribune*, October 15, 1918. Online at GenealogyBank.com. http://www.genealgybank.com/gbnk/newspapers/doc.

Fire Insurance Adjustments; Renting Rooms; Legal and Financial Aid; Lost and Found articles and telegrams; and, the Employment Bureau.[107]

There were also local places providing emergency assistance in the Fires areas. One near the northwest corner of Hermantown, near the border with Canosia Township, was established at Four Corners, where Louis Anderson's unburned farmhouse became one such aid station. It became a local gathering place too, where people with burns reached the farmhouse and took temporary shelter there, while they awaited being taken to Duluth for more extensive medical care. [108]

---

107 *Ibid.*

108 Kathryn Adams and Mary Schrock, "The 1918 Forest Fire," *Canosia Township & Pike Lake: An Illustrated History,* 1988, pp. 55-56.

# Chapter Eight: The Week After

The general outlook in the first week after the Fires, from personal accounts and newspaper articles, was portrayed as bleak. Due to the simultaneous occurrence of the fires, the Spanish Influenza Pandemic, and World War I, there was little good news to report.

With the sudden influx of deaths from outlying areas, the mortuaries in Duluth were barely able to take care of the bodies. The headline from one article summed the situation up: "Funerals Go On Day After Day. Duluth Undertaking Rooms are Scenes of Almost Continuous Services for Fire Victims." [109] Some bodies were being held for identification or to await the recovery of others in the same families. At many of the funeral parlors the funerals started early in the day, as exemplified with an 8 A.M. burial from Crawford's Morgue for an entire family, with four other funerals scheduled that same day.

Concurrently the fear of the spread of Spanish Flu led to funerals being private. Public funerals were banned, as were many other types of gatherings, by the Minnesota State Board of Health. The conditions imposed by the State Board of Health stated that, ". . . funerals of influenza victims must be private. 'Private' in the sense used by the state board means that only persons resident in the same house with the deceased and who were quarantined with the victim may attend the funeral. The caskets must be kept closed. This applies to soldiers who have died in camps as well as to civilian deaths. A minister may attend only when the embalmer in charge is present."[110]

There was a ban on gatherings at theaters, schools, and churches. The University of Minnesota was closed to ". . . civilian students until further notice. This action is necessary," the U of MN President Doctor Marion LeRoy Burton said, "because of the Spanish influenza epidemic throughout the states. Students in the colleges of medicine, pharmacy, and dentistry, because of the need of men in these professions, may attend provided they comply with the regulations laid down by the state board of health." [111]

As of the 19th of October 100 cases of Spanish Influenza had been reported in Duluth. However, it was feared that more people would become ill or die, ". . . with the crowding that has resulted through the influx of homeless. . ." because of the Fires the prior week.[112]

One unfortunate young man survived combat in World War I, only to be badly burned in the Fires while he was recuperating from his wounds at a cottage on Pike Lake. Not only was Fred Bevis wounded, he was also 'gassed' with mustard gas. He described his experience on the evening of October 12th as being "Worse than anything I saw or went through during three and a half years of fighting in France." The battles in which he fought were those of the Somme, Ypres, Lens, and Hill No. 74. [113]

The names of dead, missing, and injured known on the 19th of October occupied many columns in the local Duluth newspaper.

Transportation was also disrupted between Duluth and Superior, due to the burning of the approach to the Interstate Bridge. "Traffic between Duluth and Superior, which has been more or less impeded since the destruction of the Duluth approach to the interstate bridge, will be improved beginning this morning, by the establishment of a ferry to transport

---

109 "Funerals Go On Day after Day. Duluth Undertaking Rooms are Scenes of almost Continuous Services for Fire Victims," *Duluth News Tribune*, October 19, 1918. Online at GenealogyBank.com. http://www.genealogybank.com/doc/newspapers/image.

110 "Epidemic's Gain is Slow; Public Funerals Banner. Only Seven New Cases Reported on October 19th. Ban on Gatherings is Still Effective," *Duluth News Tribune*, October 19, 1918. Online at GenealogyBank.com. http://www.genealogybank.com/doc/newspapers/image.

111 *Ibid.*

112 *Ibid.*

113 "War Veteran is Burned Badly. Fred Bevis, Recuperating from Wounds Received in Battle, at Hospital, a Fire Victim," *Duluth News Tribune*, October 19, 1918. Online at GenealogyBank.com. http://www.genealogybank.com/doc.newspapers/image.

passengers between the [street] cars on opposite sides of the river. . .Owing to the fact that a number of Duluth [street] cars were caught on the Superior side of the bridge when the fire came, there has since been a shortage of [street] cars during the rush hours of the morning and evening in Duluth." [114]

Prisoners who were sentenced by the Court to serve terms at the work farm (the site of the current Duluth Airport) had to be taken to the county jail in Duluth. "St. Louis County Work Farm suffered several hundred dollars damages as a result of the forest fires. . .The old main camp, Superintendent Ward's and the assistant superintendent's homes, the saw mill and work shop all are burned. A total of 90 sheep also died as a result of the blaze. The new farm house and the cows and horses were saved. Several tons of hay and straw also were saved. . ." [115]

Sightseers were complicating the recovery efforts, it was reported. "Sunday sightseeing in the burned areas around Duluth is dangerous. In addition to being a waste of good time that might well be devoted to relief effort and of good gas that ought to be reserved for war use, it is tempting fate. . . . The dangerous condition existing along many of the roads throughout the burned district makes it necessary to warn everyone . . . . There are many trees burned along the roads and in a condition which will make it very easy for a slight wind to blow them across the roads. One of our men has already been killed through the falling of a tree. Furthermore there are along some of the roads, telegraph and telephone wires hanging low. One of our cars was caught by these wires and fortunately only the car was injured. Inasmuch as the ban has been raised from Sunday driving it is important that the public take notice of this extraordinary condition and that all drivers who have to go into the country exercise unusual care," Major Mullins was quoted as saying.[116]

Adding to the difficulties were profiteers who tried to take advantage of the plight of the fire sufferers, with swindling attempts. "Prompt action by Duluth's Mayor Magney appears to have stopped the buying of cattle from fire sufferers by vendors at unfair prices. The mayor yesterday declared that since he has issued his order prohibiting the buying of the livestock no reports have come to his office from any of the farmers that they had sold any of their stock. Home Guards reported that a cattle buyer came up to a widow on the Pike Lake Road. Her home and all her household goods had been burned, and she was penniless. The buyer after some argument paid her $10 for one cow. Just as he was about to leave the place with the cow, members of the Home Guard came up and asked the widow how much the man paid her for the animal and she told them. The result was that the buyer had to give the cow back, the soldiers gave the woman some money, and the man was so treated so 'nice' that he promised never to attempt to fleece anyone else." [117]

Among all the despair, a glimmer of hope appeared. A Duluthian claimed to see ". . . a rainbow arched over the devastated area at 5:30 o'clock last night. 'That may be taken as a sign of hope since we haven't had rain for some time,' he said." [118] A week too late, substantial rains finally came on the 19th of October, 1918.

---

114 "Ferry Traffic Between Ports. Street Car Company Joins with Emergency Steamer. Fares Continues Same," *Duluth News Tribune,* October 19, 1918. Online at GenealogyBank.com. http://www.genealogybank.com/gbnk/newspapers/doc.

115 "Work Farm Out of Commission. Fire Damage Compels Use of County Jail-Reconstruction Plans Not Yet Made," *Duluth News Tribune,* October 19, 1918. Online at GenealogyBank.com. http://www.genealogybank.com/doc/newspapers/image.

116 "Sunday Touring Dangerous, Says Motor Officer. Sightseeing in Burned Areas May Bring Loss of Life, Maj. H.JU. Mullin's Warning," *Duluth News Tribune,* October 19, 1918. Online at GenealogyBank.com. http://www.genealogybank.com/doc/newspapers/image.

117 "Vandal Buyers Made to Desist. Profiteers Stopped in Areas Near Duluth by Prompt Action of Mayor Magney," *Duluth News Tribune,* October 19, 1918. Online at GenealogyBank.com. http://www.genealogybank.com/doc/newspapers/image.

118 "Sees Rainbow. Hopes for Relief from Dry Weather," *Duluth News Tribune,* October 19, 1918. Online at Genealogybank.com. http://www.genealogybank.com/doc/newspapers/image.

# Chapter Nine: Reconstruction

In the first week after the Fires Governor Burnquist and a number of other state officials, including State Forester William T. Cox, traveled to inspect the fire district. The first major step was to create a state government committee authorized to deal with the situation and to coordinate the relief efforts of the several groups who had stepped in to assist in the emergency. This was done on October 16th when the Minnesota Commission of Public Safety (CPS) met in a special session in Moose Lake at the governor's request.[119] The Commission authorized both St. Louis and Carlton counties to spend all the available monies in their general revenue fund for immediate relief. More importantly, the commission created the Minnesota Fire Relief Commission that ultimately assumed overall responsibility for relief operations in the entire fire district.[120] The legislature also appropriated $1,850,000.00 for the commission on February 7, 1919, but only after debate and a visit to the fire area by the relevant legislative committees.[121]

The commission decided at its first meetings that some permanent or long-term relief measures were necessary if the region would ever recover and return to some semblance of normal, pre-fire living. Its philosophy was to "help every man to help himself," and to that end it formed a Central Replacement Committee with four district committees in St. Louis, northern and southern Carlton, and Aitkin counties. These district groups, made up of local people, scrutinized applications for assistance and listened to appeals.[122] To this organization were added local committees from the destroyed communities. Offices and warehouses were established in 11 towns, and in 12 smaller communities temporary distribution centers were operated.[123]

The commission provided food rations which enabled people to do their own cooking rather than depend on public mess halls run by the military or the Red Cross. Refugees were also given lumber, hardware, and furnishings to make a small shelter. Plans were immediately drafted for two styles—a small 12-by-16-foot structure for small families and a larger 12-by-20-foot building for bigger families. Elaborate forms had to be filled out to prove loss and show that one had no significant resources, but the supplies to construct these shelters were quick in coming, with the result that people returning to the area in October and November of 1918 were able to have at least a crude and sparse structure to call "home" within a few days of their arrival.[124] Later in 1918 state appropriations enabled people to put siding on the shelters and to make them more comfortable.[125] The Special Collection Archives of the Kathryn Martin Library at UMD has a file with blueprints, lists of materials, and a written description of the Red Cross houses and barns, which has been copied hereto in its entirety.

---

119 Francis Carroll and Franklin Raiter, "At the Time of Our Misfortune: Relief Efforts Following the Cloquet Fire of 1918," *Minnesota Historical Society Magazine, Fall, 1983, p. 277. http://collections.mnhs.org/MNHistoryMagazine/articles/48/v48i07p270-282.pdf*
120 *Ibid.*, page 278.
121 *Ibid.*, page 278.
122 *Ibid.*, page 278.
123 *Ibid.*, page 279.
124 *Ibid.*, page 279.
125 *Ibid.*, page 279.

## "DESCRIPTIONS OF HOUSES AND BARNS
## FURNISHED UNDER THE PLAN OF THE RECONSTRUCTION COMMITTEE.

The barns are all 12 feet wide and either 10, 12, 14, 16, 17, 20, 22, or 24 feet long. They have no floors and the walls rest on 4x6 sills. On these sills are placed 2x4 studding 2 feet apart. The studs are 3 feet long on the low side and 10 feet long on the high side. On top of the studs along the sides are placed 2x4 plates. The studs are braced by 1x6 boards. The rafters are 2x6, 14 feet long and the rafters are covered with shiplap and tarred felt held in place with lath. The walls are of shiplap inside and outside of studding. A door is to be built on one end and windows are provided on one side.

Houses are of two styles, No. 1 and No. 2. Number 1 is 12x16 in size. The sills are of 2 pieces of 2x8 along each side. These rest on posts made of 2x12 timbers. 2x8 joists run across the building 2 feet apart and on these joists are laid one inch rough boards, then 2x4 plates are laid upon which are to be erected 2x4 studding on 16 inch centers. A 2x4 plate is placed on top of the studding. The studdings are braced with 2x4 bracing cut to fit in between the studding and are shown on the plans furnished. The rafters are of 2 x 4, 8 feet long, 16 inches apart. On the rafters are placed shiplap and roofing paper, the outside of studding is then to be covered with one-half inch insulite, a prepared frost-proof wallboard coming in sheets. This insulite is fastened with large head nails. The rough floor is then to be covered with number 2 tar felt and 6 inch pine flooring , then the inside of the studding is to be covered with insulite the same as the outside. In putting up the studding tie the studding together at the top with 4 - 2x4 collar ties. A door is provided for one end and one window on each of the other sides.

Number 2 house is the same in construction as number one except that number two is 12x20 in size.

In starting any of these buildings the workman should first lay out the building for the size furnished and should not cut any material until they are sure what they are doing."[126]

The listing of supplies was quite detailed.

126 1918 Forest Fire Documents, Item 2: Standard Houses and Barns, Archives and Special Collections, Kathryn A. Martin Library, University of Minnesota, Duluth. (S6057).

IMMEDIATE RELIEF LUMBER ORDER

This material is delivered to you for immediate relief. If, after investigation, your circumstances do not warrant free material, you will be required to pay for this at cost price.

LUMBER BILL

House #1 12 x 16

| | | | | | | |
|---|---|---|---|---|---|---|
| 2 pc | 2" | x 12' | 12-0 Footing & Steps. | | | |
| 4 | 2 | 8 | 16-0 Sills & Sides. | | | |
| 11 | 2 | 8 | 12-0 Joists | | | |
| 8 | 2 | 4 | 12-0 Collar Ties. | | | |
| 55 | 2 | 4 | 8 -0 Studds | | | |
| 18 | 2 | 4 | 8 -0 Rafters | | | |
| 4 | 2 | 4 | 16-0 Plates & Shoe | | | |
| 350 Ft. | (BM) | | #4 8' Shiplap | | | |
| 220 | (BM) | | #4 Boards | 16-0 | | |
| 240 | (BM) | | #3 6' Flooring | 16-0 | | |
| 4 Pc | 1 x 6 | | 16-0 | #3 | S2S | Cornice |
| 2 | 1 x 3 | | 10 -0 | #3 | S2S | " |
| 6 | 1 x 3 | | 8 -0 | #3 | S2S | " |
| 5 | 1 x 2 | | 16-0 Battons | | | |
| 8 | 1 x 2 | | 12-0 " | | | |
| 3 Windows & Frame | | | | | | |
| 1 Door & Frame | | | | | | |

NAILS

23# 6d Nails for Insulite

32# 8d Nails

15# 20d Nails

10# 40d Nails

1 Lock 110 C

1 Pair Butts 731½
3½ x 3½

1 Galv. Roof Saddle

1 Roll Tarred Felt

3 rolls Roofing

32 Pcs. 4/0X9/0 Insulite

I accept this under the above conditions,

Station______________________________

Dated______________________________

SIGNED______________________________

[127]

127 *Ibid.*

While both urban and rural groups were eligible for the same kind of food, shelter, and clothing assistance, the commission soon decided that farmers would need more help if they were to get back on their feet. A farmer, it was reasoned, required shelter not only for his family, but also for his farm animals and crops. The commission therefore provided lumber for the construction of barns and outbuildings appropriate to the kind and size of farm that had been destroyed by the fire. Lost farm implements and equipment also had to be replaced. Furthermore, the surviving farm animals had to be fed and, because the hay and feed had been destroyed by the fire, these too were provided by the commission. For those who had lost all of their animals, the relief group attempted to make a start at replacing them. The United States Department of Agriculture, the University of Minnesota, and the state Guernsey and the Holstein Breeder's Association helped in this by giving assistance and lending prize animals to reproduce decimated herds. The commission also provided the seeds for various crops in the spring of 1919 so that the whole farm economy could begin functioning again.[128]

However, compensation did not come quickly enough for some people. Quite a few fire refugees argued that if they had received what was owed them sooner they would have become independent and not had to rely on others for as long a period of time. Disgruntled letters continued to flow to various authorities into 1919.[129]

There were also special situations with which the commission had to deal. Many people who were burned or injured remained in hospitals for prolonged periods of time. Fire-related medical necessities were almost immediately overtaken by the influenza epidemic, which fell particularly hard upon an area where people were living in crowded and inadequate circumstances at the onset of a cold and rainy autumn. In the fire area, influenza became part of the misery of the whole experience, but it was left for the commission, together with the Red Cross and the Home Guard, to deal with it medically as part of the disaster.[130]

Governor Burnquist issued an appeal for public support, asking people to send money to either the Commission of Public Safety or the Relief Commission. "I cannot urge too strongly," he said, "upon the people of the State, the immediate necessity of large funds to care for the personal needs of those suffering and to aid in restoring the settlements that have been destroyed." Those who had survived the fire and lost homes or family needed the support and sympathy of the rest of the state, the governor pleaded. The state responded to his appeal.[131] Money came from towns, clubs, churches, schools, and merchants. Most of the checks were accompanied with expressions of sympathy and encouragement, and they came from every part of the nation.[132] Prince Axel of Denmark conveyed his concern to Burnquist less than a week after the disaster; governors of other states sent official condolences and offers of help, frequently adding private contributions of their own.[133]

---

128 Francis Carroll and Franklin Raiter, *Op. cit.*,p. 279.
129 *Ibid.*, p. 280.
130 *Ibid.*, p. 280.
131 *Ibid.*, p.280.
132 *Ibid.*, p. 281.
133 *Ibid.*, p. 281.

# Chapter Ten: Years of Legal and Political Wrangling

Once immediate needs had been dealt with, long term matters needed to be considered, specifically the matter of who, or what, was responsible for the Fires. Politics reared its ugly head into the area of responsibility and blame, as well as to who would be required to make reparations for the resultant death and destruction from the Fires.

A commonly held belief was that the railroads were responsible. In the early days of 1919 lawsuits began to be filed in the Minnesota Courts. As Carroll and Raiter state, "These suits eventually involved millions of dollars, a partial settlement authorized by President Warren G. Harding, and a legal battle that lasted until 1935."[134]

During World War I most of the railroads in the United States had been nationalized by the Federal government, in order to coordinate rail traffic across the nation in wartime. To that end, Congress created the Railroad Administration. One of the terms of the legislation was that the Railroad Administration had to obey the laws and the courts of the state in which it operated. Lawsuits that arose against local railroads eventually named the director general of the Railroad Administration as an agent of the president. The legal office of the administration continued to operate into the 1930s, although the railroads themselves were restored to their original companies in 1920.

The Minnesota State Forester, William Cox, was the state official in charge of forests, including monitoring forest conditions and attempting to control fires. His report about the fires was submitted to the governor on November 1, 1918, only two and a half weeks after the conflagration. Obviously sufficient time was not taken to evaluate or study the conditions in the vast burned over areas. Cox blamed the Fires upon marsh fires; small fires started by travelers, railroad locomotives, and landowners; and, an insufficient number of forest rangers and trained firefighters. In his estimation, the most important factor in the severity and wide-spread nature of the Fires was the inadequate funding appropriated by the Minnesota legislature.

At the urging of Cox, Governor Burnquist appointed a Forest Fire Investigation Committee, chaired by Duluth corporate and railroad lawyer Jed Washburn, plus six others of varying backgrounds. This commission began holding hearings on November 14th, 1918, in Duluth, Moose Lake, and Cloquet. They also traveled throughout the fire district. Again, the hearings were done quite quickly, and a report was sent to Governor Burnquist on November 26, 1918. The Commission listed the reasons for the Fires as the dryness of the season; the scant rainfall; the drainage of swamps; the accumulation of slash; simmering fires in bogs and swamps that got out of hand; and to a rather small extent, railroad operations. Mainly the catastrophe was ascribed to be an act of God.[135]

The railroads became alarmed at the conclusions and began to prepare to fight the aspersions of blame that they feared would be coming their way, in the form of legal liability and lawsuits. The Railroad Administration started its own investigation in January of 1919, along the Great Northern line northwest of Cloquet, near Milepost 62. By early February of 1919 the Railroad Administration lawyers were becoming alarmed, fearing that the investigations would attract attention to the matter of possible railroad responsibility. They also feared the involvement of local lawyers who would sue the railroads on a contingency fee basis. Eventually all the railroads operating in the burned-over areas sent investigators out into the field, to take statements from the survivors about the characteristics of the fire and the property destroyed. The reams of written statements were gathered into books brought into trials and used against many of the same people when they testified in the lawsuits. If the testimony given at the trial varied from that taken down by the railroad investigators, the railroad lawyers read the earlier contradictory statements to the court.[136]

---

134 Francis M. Carroll and Franklin R. Raiter, "Fire in the Courts," *Fires of Autumn; The Cloquet-Moose Lake Disaster of 1918*,_ Minnesota Historical Society Press, St. Paul, MN, 1990, page 130.
135 *Ibid.*, p. 131.
136 *Ibid.*, p. 133.

Attorney N. B. Arnold and his attorney brother, John B. Arnold, were asked to seek compensation on a case-by-case basis, starting in late 1918. As Arnold investigated along the Great Northern rail line in the Brookston area, he found more farmers who had evidence that the fires could be traced to the railroads. They wanted to sue to recover for their losses, and approached the firm of Arnold & Arnold to represent them.

The earliest court cases resulted in mixed success, with some trials favoring the railroads and a few others the private individuals. Within the next two years 15,003 cases were brought against the various railroads in the fire region and against the Railroad Administration. The numbers of cases convinced the officials that they were ". . . being made the victims of unscrupulous northern Minnesota lawyers who had traveled through the burned-over country drumming up business."[137] Of necessity, most of the cases had been taken on a contingent fee basis, rather than cash before the trials. The fire victims generally had no cash, and could not pay legal fees up front.

The legal cases involved a tremendous amount of legal preparation, including hiring timber cruisers from 1919 to 1921 to inspect the areas burned and estimate the value of timber and land destroyed by the fires. (A *timber cruiser* is a logger who makes a survey or sampling of standing trees to estimate their volume, product class, size, quality, and/or financial value.)[138]

At one time the paperwork involved in compiling evidence, filing suits, and corresponding with litigants required twenty-three clerks and stenographers in Cloquet, and fifteen in Duluth.[139]

A group was established in 1919: the Northern Minnesota Fire Sufferers Association. Its purpose was to raise money to pay plaintiff's legal fees; lobby for fair settlements; and act as a clearing house. Eventually it had seven thousand members.[140]

The Northern Minnesota Fire Sufferers Association complained that the railroads harassed the people and tried to discourage fire sufferers from pursuing any reparations. By early 1920 the Railroad Administration had conducted its own investigations with the purpose of collecting evidence that could be used in court to deny the claim of the fire sufferers. The Railroad Administration's legal division looked upon the fire sufferers association as a tool of unscrupulous and greedy Minnesota lawyers.

A major trial of an aggregate of some 278 Cloquet cases before a panel of five judges was held in the Hibbing Courthouse, from May 9, 1920, through July 9, 1920. Judge William A. Cant of Duluth issued Findings stating the railroad had allowed much combustible material to accumulate along its tracks and sidings. Insufficient patrolmen were deployed along the tracks by the railroads, he continued. Furthermore, a locomotive had started the Fires in this area at Milepost 62.[141] Not surprisingly, the Railroad Administration appealed the case to the Minnesota Supreme Court. The Supreme Court issued its affirmation on July 22, 1921, agreeing with the lower court and its decision. This decision was regarded as a legal victory for Cloquet fire claimants.

Fortunately, the handwritten notes in the Board of Township of Herman Supervisors large record books survived the Fires. In a meeting from February 13, 1922, a motion was made for the township to file a claim against the U. S. Government for town property lost in the Fire of October 12, 1918, such as culverts, plows, scrapers, shovels, and iron scythes and all other property destroyed by said fire belonging to the Town of Herman. Arnold and Arnold, Attorneys, were instructed to bring suit against the U. S. Government in the name of the Township of Herman, St. Louis County, Minnesota.[142]

---

137 *Ibid.*, page 134.
138 http://ncforestry.info/ncdfr/glossary_of_forest_management-terms/ (Accessed 11-27-2017)
139 Frances M. Carroll and Franklin R. Raiter, Op. cit., page 135.
140 *Ibid.*, page 135.
141 *Ibid.*, page 141.
142 Photocopy of Township book entry courtesy of Bette Grussendorf of the Hermantown Historical Society. Originals are retained at the Minnesota Historical Society in St. Paul, MN.

Individual law suits began to be filed in ever increasing numbers. Both sides came to the conclusion that the courts in the fire areas could not deal with the flood of claims. Judge Cant proposed that Congress, in cooperation with the Railroad Administration, "provide for a commission, or possibly a few groups of commissioners, who shall take this matter in hand and speedily determine who is entitled to recover and how much."[143]

Railroad Administration staff, chiefly James Davis, proposed a blanket settlement for the Cloquet fire sufferers: a payment of 50 percent of the amount claimed for the 278 litigated cases and 40 percent of the amount claimed for the remaining 2,600 Cloquet cases as yet untried. Davis viewed the Fires as an Act of God, and therefore no legal liability was able to be established. Much to the despair of the fire sufferers, they were essentially told, in Davis' own words uttered years later, "'Gentlemen, this is the best I can do; take it or leave it.' If they preferred to take 50 per cent in cash, I did not deprive them of any legal right. They had their choice. If that is coercion, there was coercion."[144]

This was essentially the settlement reluctantly agreed to by the people of Cloquet. As Carroll and Raiter stated "It was a bitter and disillusioning experience, which seemed to reveal the iron fist of government exercised against essentially defenseless citizenry... After judgments had been made by the district court for dollar amounts to be paid by the administration, no move was made to pay them, although the trial stipulations formed an agreement to pay if the administration was found liable. Instead, the administration came forward with the 'take it or leave it' settlement offer of 50 percent."[145]

The Cloquet settlement set the pattern for resolution of most of the claims in other burned-over areas. New suits for damages from the railroads for fires that burned along the outskirts of Duluth right down to the eastern edge of the city and to Lake Superior began to be filed in late 1923. Several of these went on to jury trials which the fire sufferers won. Predictably, the Railroad Administration appealed the decisions, and again the lower court decisions were reaffirmed. On March 28, 1925, James Davis made an offer of settlement for the cases pending in the region north of Duluth on the eastern perimeter of the fire, with a maximum payment of 50 and 40 percent in two zones.

The Railroad Administration ended up paying 42.7 percent of the amount determined by the courts. The administration had also arranged for claimants who had settled to sign waivers to protect it from further law suits from fire sufferers. Again, in the words of Raiter and Carroll, "Thus, although the administration had repeatedly lost in the Minnesota courts, as a federal government agency it refused to be forced to comply with the rulings and judgments of the Minnesota courts, though this may have been in violation of the federal legislation creating the Railroad Administration."[146]

However, James Davis thought it was way too generous a settlement. To him, the people of northern Minnesota never had any question that the fires had been simply an act of God until the local lawyers convinced them that their losses could be made good through suits against the Railroad Administration. The local attorneys, he believed, would be the chief beneficiaries of any financial settlements.[147]

To the weary fire sufferers, the settlement was a betrayal. To Judge Herbert A. Dancer, the settlement ". . . was a cheap settlement for the Government."[148]

In 1928 a new group, the Minnesota Forest Fire Reimbursement Association, was organized to lobby Congress and to bring pressure from all over the nation to support a congressional solution to the problem. It hoped to be more successful in obtaining a fair settlement than the courts had been. One of the group's leaders was Cloquet lawyer Frank Yetka, who started a national campaign. In April of 1928 the first bill was sponsored by Congressman William Carss and Senator Henrik Shipstead to obtain payment of the unpaid balance of the fire suffers' adjudicated claims against the Railroad Adminis-

143 Francis Carroll and Franklin Raiter, Op. cit., p.145.
144 *Ibid.*, p.150.
145 *Ibid.*, p. 151.
146 *Ibid.*, p. 155.
147 *Ibid.*, p.155.
148 *Ibid.*, p.158.

tration. The bill was never reported from committee. Nevertheless, when William Pittenger of Duluth succeeded Carss in 1928 as representative from Minnesota's Eighth Congressional District, he too, with the support of Senator Shipstead, fought to have the bill reintroduced. [149]

At least Pittinger's re-introduction of the bill resulted in public hearings that gave the fire sufferers access to a national platform to explain the fire and the injustices they had suffered at the hands of the Railroad Administration. Pittinger's bill was introduced on December 2, 1929, then referred to the Committee on Claims, then to a subcommittee. Hearings were held from March 26 to 29, 1930, with James Davis vigorously opposing Pittinger's bill.[150] Davis said that the Minnesotans were victims of a purely natural disaster and had already gotten more from the Railroad Administration than they really deserved. Davis urged the Congress to not give the fire sufferers any more aid. Behind the scenes, he used his connections and influence in the White House to undermine the Pittinger Bill, going to President Herbert Hoover's secretary. [151]

The Minnesota Forest Fire Reimbursement Association sent several people who testified at the hearings, foremost among them being Judge Herbert Dancer. Judge Dancer's main point was that the Railroad Administration had violated its congressional mandate and the Minnesota law by ignoring the findings and decisions of the Minnesota courts, on all levels. He concluded that Davis had no right to disobey Minnesota law simply because he disagreed with it. Three attorneys also testified in favor of the Pittinger Bill: N. B. Arnold, who handled cases in Cloquet-Alborn-Brookston areas; Victor J. Michaelson of Cloquet, who took cases from both the Cloquet and Moose Lake areas; and Theodore Hollister of Duluth, the main lawyer on the cases north and east of Duluth. Three fire sufferers also testified eloquently for Pittinger's bill: Frank Yetka, a Cloquet lawyer; Carl D. Ohman, a Cloquet businessman; and Anna Dickie Olesen, a well-known Chautauqua speaker and the first woman to run for the United States Senate from the Democractic party.[152] (*Chautauqua* refers to various traveling shows and local assemblies that flourished in the U.S. in the late 19th and early 20th centuries that gave popular education combined with entertainment in the form of lectures, concerts, and plays, and were modeled after the Chautauqua Institution of Western New York.)[153]

As a result of the subcommittee hearings, reports were made to the Committee on Claims on June 30, 1930, recommending that the entire Committee on Claims make a decision on the Pittinger Bill. On the morning of January 16, 1931, the bill finally came before the entire Committee on Claims. After several hours, the chairman referred the Pittinger bill to an executive session of the Committee on Claims which met January 18, 1931. As a result the original bill was amended and recommended for passage. Despite the favorable recommendation, through 1930 and 1931 efforts were made to enlist the support of the Hoover administration of the Pittenger Bill, to little avail. Congressional correspondence was sent to President Hoover, who in turn forwarded the materials to Secretary of the Treasury and Director of the Railroad Administration, Andrew W. Mellon. Mr. Mellon passed this material to Assistant Director General Sidney F. Andrews, who had prepared the Railroad Administration's briefs against the Congressional hearings. Andrews advised President Hoover on May 26, 1930, that the bill should not be passed, quoting extensively from James Davis' remarks. Private appeals to the president were politely turned down by White House staff.[154]

The Pittinger bill failed to get the unanimous consent of the House of Representatives and died with the expiration of the Seventy-first Congress. An undaunted Congressman Pittinger reintroduced the bill on December 8, 1931. Again it was sent to the Committee on Claims, now under the control of the Democrats. Another report was issued by the Committee on Claims, with split opinions down party lines, with Republicans opposed to it and Democrats favoring the

149 *Ibid.*, p. 159.
150 *Ibid.*, p. 160.
151 *Ibid.*, p. 161.
152 *Ibid.*, pp. 163-164.
153 "Chautauqua" defined by on-line Merriam-Webster Dictionary, https://merriam-webster.com/dictionary/chautauqua (Accessed 11-27-2017)
154 Francis M. Carroll and Franklin Raiter, Op. cit. p. 166.

Pittinger bill. Senator Henrik Shipstead introduced a parallel bill in the Senate, but progress in both the House of Representatives and the Senate came to a halt.

Pittinger reported that a problem blocking consideration of fire reparations was that claims as large as the fire sufferers' ran contrary to the economy drive with which the Hoover Administration hoped to ease the Great Depression. The administration was urged to support the new Pittinger bill, but the White House staff avoided any involvement with the bill, and President Hoover never commented publicly on the claims bill or signed a letter himself. On June 1, 1932, on the floor of the House, Congressman Thomas L. Blanton of Texas objected to the bill because of the expense it would make to the depleted treasury. Yet another time Pittinger's bill was removed from the private calendar on which unanimous consent of the House of Representatives was required.[155]

Early in 1933, with the assembling of the New Deal Administration under President Franklin Delano Roosevelt, Frank Yetka wrote to the entire Minnesota contingent in the House and Senate on behalf of the Minnesota Forest Fire Reimbursement Association. However, in the emergency session of Congress called by President Roosevelt the Committee on Claims had not even been organized. Shortly thereafter Arthur Mullen, a key Roosevelt supporter, was hired as a lobbyist in Washington to forward the interests of the Minnesota Forest Fire Reimbursement Association. From time to time delegations from Minnesota went to Washington to present the fire sufferers' case in various offices.

Frank Yetka and Howard T. Abbot, a member of a prominent Duluth law firm, drafted a thirteen page letter to be sent to President Roosevelt over the governor's signature. It summarized the entire situation, including the actions of the courts and the Railroad Administration. It urged the president to support the passage of the current measure. Senator Shipstead delivered the letter in person. President Roosevelt referred it to Attorney General Homer Cummings, who on December 27, 1933, responded. He also gave the president a brief account of the fire and the litigation. President Roosevelt sent letters to the chairmen of the House and Senate claims committees on January 24, 1934, quoting the attorney general's view that the subject should be looked at further.[156]

Although things finally looked promising, there was no immediate success looming. Again the bill was considered and debated, and eventually the bill died in committee with the expiration of the Seventy-third Congress. Although Minnesotans appealed to the White House for support of the bill, their last minute requests were met with polite sympathy.[157]

Shortly after the new Seventy-fourth Congress met, the bill was again introduced to obtain compensation for the Minnesota fire claimants. Eventually the bill was included in an omnibus claims bill in the House, and President Roosevelt instructed his staff to monitor the situation and to ask Congressman Kvale if he needed help. Minnesota Governor Olson kept in touch with the White House by telegraph. Even then there was resistance from the floor of the House. Congressman Pittenger gave a short history of the plight of the fire sufferers and the succession of bills that had been attempted. The result was that the fire sufferers' bill remained in the omnibus claims bill and was passed later that day. President Roosevelt signed the bill on August 27, 1935.[158]

When the bill was finally signed into law the matter was transferred to the Treasury Department for their staff to manage the payment of the actual claims. By September 13, 1935, the comptroller general announced the procedure by which claims could be made. The Treasury Department used the Railroad Administration's account records for agreed-upon amounts of each eligible claim accepted in the early 1920s. In 1935, the task remained simply to verify the claim, calculate the remainder to be paid, and locate the claimant or survivor. The Minnesota Forest Fire Reimbursement Association helped the government by sending Ralph E. Burdick, its legal advisor, to Washington to help provide information.

---

155 *Ibid.*, p. 167.
156 *Ibid.*, p. 170.
157 *Ibid.*, p. 171.
158 *Ibid.*, p. 172.

There he was joined by Congressman Pittenger; Hartford Cox, one of the lawyers who had worked with the cases since 1919; and Frank Yetka, now the Minnesota State Insurance Commissioner. A large staff of Treasury Department auditors and clerks processed the claims, and the first checks were sent out by mid-November.

Carroll and Raiter aptly summed it up. "It was a great triumph for the victims of the fire of 1918. For the first time in a forest fire disaster, a substantial proportion of the fire sufferers had been able to successfully sue in the courts for damages traceable to railroad origins. Openly defied by the Railroad Administration in the 1920s, the fire sufferers, their lawyers, and the elected officials of the state had, after more than ten years of struggle, passed their claims victoriously in the halls of Congress."[159]

159 *Ibid.*, p. 174.

# Chapter Eleven: Things Would Never Be the Same

Residents of towns and farms alike saw the fruits of their years of labors burned to ashes in a few moments, leaving them virtually destitute. Yet, as Richardson says, "In spite of all the misery and loss a fine courage and a general optimism prevailed. . ."[160]

A little less than a month after the Fires, the 11th hour of the 11th day of the 11th month was observed with weary relief and thanksgiving. At least one of the three tragedies of the year 1918, the First World War, had officially come to an end. Now they had to survive the onslaught of the Spanish Influenza pandemic, and go on after the Fire had destroyed their world. The stability of the classroom and school could not be counted upon for all. With some families departing the area for a short period of time, others leaving permanently, and the deaths of some students, the Hermantown schools and classes would never be the same. The population of Hermantown in the 1920 Federal census was 842, down from 925 in 1910.[161]

Three of the schools in the township burned down: the McKinley School, located near the intersection of the Five Corners Road and the Maple Grove Road, just east of the Midway Road; the Roosevelt School, located at the intersection of the Rose Road and Midway Road; and the Lincoln School at Adolph, near the Midway Road and Duluth, Missabe and Northern Railway track. The only building left standing at Five Corners was the Immanuel Lutheran Church, in which classes were held for two years afterwards, while a new McKinley School was built at the intersection of West Arrowhead Road and Midway Road. The Roosevelt School was not replaced, and children who had formerly attended that school attended the larger McKinley School built after the Fires. The Lincoln School at Adolph was rebuilt.[162]

The North Star Creamery was built at Five Corners by local farmers in the 1900s. However, it never opened its doors because the 1918 Fire destroyed it, according to local historian Art Fichtner. [163]

According to Mr. Fichtner, the sawmill that had been owned by Mr. Soderholm at Adolph was sold by Mrs. Soderholm after her husband's death in 1914, and in about 1916 was moved by J.M. Castonquay to the area at the intersection of Maple Grove Road and Lavaque Road. It too was destroyed in the Fires.[164]

The Adolph general store, opened by pioneer resident Adolph Bjorlin in 1892, as well as the post office established the following year in the rear of the store, were wiped out.

The oldest church in the entire township that was built in 1890, commonly known as St. Paul's Evangelical German Church, was destroyed. Once again the congregation did not have a church building close to their homes in Hermantown. The main body, of which the Hermantown branch was an affiliate, was in downtown Duluth on Tenth Avenue East, a considerable distance to travel especially during inclement weather on marginal roads. Several years later it was rebuilt on land donated by the Ruhnke family, just a little east and across the road from its original location on the north side of the Hermantown Road near the where it intersects the Lavaque Road. It was located diagonally from the original church site. Later the church building was sold, and then converted into an apartment sometime in the 1960s. Today, the Peace United Church of Christ located in the Kenwood area of Duluth is the inheritor of that early Hermantown congregation.[165]

Not unlike their German Lutheran counterparts, the congregation of the Hermantown Lutheran Church lost their

---

160 H.W. Richardson, "The Northeastern Minnesota Forest Fires of October 12, 1918," *Geographical Review*, vol. no. 4 (April, 1919), page 227. *JSTOR, JSTOR*, www.jstor.org/stable/207371.

161 "A History of Hermantown," *Hermantown Star, City of Quality Living*, April, 1989, page 5.

162 Information on schools comes from the investigative efforts of Bette Grussendorf and Delaine Carlson of the Hermantown Historical Society, through e-mail and conversations stretching over a period of years.

163 Art Fichtner, et. al., *Hermantown, 1874 -1976. A History of Hermantown as Remembered by Its Citizens*, by Book Committee of the Hermantown Hockey Auxiliary.

164 Art Fichtner, et. al., Op.cit.

165 William Kohlts, e-mail message to Delaine Carlson, dated December 1, 2017.

This photo of the St. Paul's Evangelical German Church photo is courtesy of the Hermantown Historical Society. With all of the trees around it is surmised to be the church before the 1918 Fires.
*Information about the St. Paul's Evangelical German Church is courtesy of William Kohlts of the Peace United Church of Christ.*

chapel built on the grounds of Bethany Cemetery in 1914, to the 1918 Fires. They met in the home of William Engwall until 1924, when a church was built on ground donated by Mr. Engwall, and was renamed and reorganized into Salem Lutheran Church. [166]

Where Railroad tracks and the roads crossed marshlands, rivers, creeks, and small rivulets, transportation was rendered impossible, due to burned wooden culverts and bridges. By the latter half of the twentieth century metal culverts and steel bridges spanned wet and lowlands, replacing wooden structures. The many bridges and culverts that needed to be replaced or repaired slowed relief work. Rural mail routes, with letters being the major communication means of the day, suffered great delays until transportation was gradually restored. [167]

The effects of the Fires upon the soil were mixed. Where the Fires did not burn long and hot, the soils were judged to have been enriched by large quantities of burned vegetation, especially wood, with wood ash supplying beneficial potash content. However, where the fires lingered and were particularly intense, especially in peat bogs and marshlands, the soil

166 Art Fichtner, et. al., Op. cit.
167 H.W. Richardson, Op. cit, p. 227.

was virtually sterilized and regeneration was slower. Even today in some places, layers in the soil show the burning from the 1918 Fires. In 2011 Carlton County Archaeologist Steven Blondo remarked, "There is a marker within the soil that does date to the 1918 Fire . . . everything you find below (that layer) is pre-1918, and everything above it is after 1918." [168] Local farmers in adjoining Canosia township stated the fire had burned deeply into the ground: . . . "down to the rock." Another resident remarked, "It destroyed the land so bad." [169]

The farmers suffered enormous loss, with many horses, cattle, pigs, poultry, and wild game such as deer and rabbits being burned to death. Richardson said that ". . .even fish in some of the shallower streams are reported killed."[170] In some cases poultry, pigs, dogs, cattle, or horses were found ". . .wandering disconsolately about the ruins of their former comfortable domiciles. How under the circumstances any of these animals escaped unscathed is one of the mysteries." [171]

In the Township of Herman Board of Supervisors meeting held March 31, 1919, the Supervisors felt compelled to take action on the disposal of dead livestock. "On motion the Clerk was instructed to notify the Fire Relief Commission to see that all dead cattle around the Community barns in the Township of Herman be buried." [172]

The action recommended at the spring meeting seems to contradict the optimistic tone taken by a newspaper article from two weeks after the Fires. Plans for shelters for livestock as well as horses were detailed. One week after the Fires four 85-foot barns were in the process of actual construction, being built at the rate of one a day by a crew of both hired and voluntary carpenters and laborers.

The St. Louis County commissioners met in emergency sessions every night the first week after the Fires, to arrange for and direct details of emergency road work and livestock shelters. On the 24th of October, 1918, the seventh of a group of barns for livestock centers was started. Each center where large enough unburned buildings were not available, two temporary structures were built; one to house dry cows and young stock; and a second being a dairy barn for 36 milk cows. The barns were built as quickly and economically as possible, with walls and roofs of shiplap, covered with roofing paper. Their purpose was to house the cattle temporarily until individual farmers were able to take care of their stock on their own farms. These centers were established at the following locations throughout southern St. Louis County: Commissioner Swanstrom's tool-house; Commissioner Little's tool-house; Commissioner Beck's tool-house; Widde's barn; Adolph; Munger; St. Louis County Work Farm; Twig; Pike Lake; Brookston; Sunset Lake; St. Louis County Poor Farm; Woodland Dairy; and Culver. Horse barns had already been provided, at the West End livery and another at the Morgan Park company barns. However, the communities housing livestock centers were apparently responsible for caring for the animals housed there. With people trying to get reestablished themselves, it was difficult to enlist people to care for animals at a community facility.

Richardson noted that "In some of the outlying settlements timber wolves were later reported as becoming numerous and destructive to remaining and unprotected livestock." [173]

A pathetic story of an old horse, roaming the streets of Duluth in the spring of 1919, was written in the Duluth News Tribune. "Old, Lame and Gray, Refugee Horse Waits for his Master. No doubt he wore out his patient life struggling in the tilling of some settler's hard acres. Then came the great fire of Oct. 12 and he followed the stream of refugees into Duluth. Since that time he has wandered the streets, shelterless and starving. He's only an old, lame, gray horse, blind in one eye. Yesterday John G. Ross found him at Mesaba Avenue and Fourth Street. His gray hair was half a foot long and he

---

168 Jana Peterson, "Carlton County Archaeologist makes his living rediscovering the past," Duluth News Tribune, July 6, 2011.
169 Kathryn Adams and Mary Schrock, "The Forest Fire of 1918," *Canosia Township & Pike Lake: An Illustrated History,* 1988, p. 56.
170 H.W. Richardson, Op.cit.,p. 228.
171 H.W. Richardson, Op. cit., p. 229.
172 Photocopy of township books courtesy of Bette Grussendorf of the Hermantown Historical Society. The original Board of Supervisors Books are retained at the Minnesota State Historical Society in St. Paul.
173 H.W. Richardson, Op. cit., p. 228.

could scarce walk. Residents of the vicinity stated that he first appeared after the fire and had been in the neighborhood since—one refugee uncared for. He was taken to the Twin Ports barns yesterday and is being held until someone claims him. Unless he is taken soon he will be humanely destroyed. Who is his master?"[174]

Family pets did not fare too well either. Some families did take their pets with them as they fled. Unfortunately, others could not find the terrified pets that went into hiding. As the title of an article starkly remarked, "Dogs Stick to Thresholds; Perish While on Duty." Reports received in Duluth said… "Charred and burned bodies and skeletons of many of the pet Fidos, Tiges, and Sheps were found near or in the ruins of the homes in the burned district. Where the dogs were separated by the smoke and fire from the rest of the family, it was shown by the location at the charred remains of the dogs that in many cases the pets had returned to the homes and perished with them." [175]

The community livestock centers began to be auctioned off in the middle of 1919. By that August a Duluth News Tribune article reported the sale of a Hermantown community barn and bunkhouse to Hermantown resident Charles Velander, for $300 and $200 respectively. Mr. Velander's bid was approved by the St. Louis County Board of Commissioners on August 12, 1919. The other community barns and bunkhouses, with the exception of the buildings at the St. Louis County Work Farm, would be put up for bid and sold thereafter. (The buildings at the Work Farm were turned over to the Work Farm Commission.) [176]

Countless official records were destroyed. The agricultural and farming clubs had a successful history in all parts of the township. However, the Jackson Farmer's Club, "…believing that it would be interesting and valuable in years to come to have a permanent record of the club's activities since it was first organized, decided to appoint a committee to prepare a history of the club. B. C. Ericksen, J. W. Johnson, and Fred Ward were appointed to do this work. The committee was confronted with the fact that all records prior to the fall of 1918 were destroyed in the great forest fire that swept this and surrounding neighborhoods on October 12, 1918. The records were again destroyed when the home of our secretary, Mr. J. W. Johnson, was burned June 30, 1919. In trying to save the Club and other records Mr. Johnson nearly lost his life. The Committee therefore decided to call together as many as possible of the old timers who had a hand in the early development of the Club and from their memory compile the facts. On the evening of May 30, 1928, the following folks met at the County Work Farm for this purpose: Mr. Chris Ugstad, Mr. & Mrs. B. C. Ericksen, Mr. & Mrs. J. O. Erickson, Ed Bye, Adolph Abrahamson, Mr. & Mrs. Fred Ward, Chas. Sampson, P.A. Paulson, and J. W. Johnson. The committee is indebted also for information furnished by Mr. Ole Larson, Mr. Emil Johnson, Mr. John Emil Anderson, and others."[177]

Three of the members of the Jackson Farmer's Club who were noted to have fought in the First World War were Dave Johnson, who entered the Navy but died of the "flu" January 4, 1919; Olaf Ugstad, who entered the Spruce Division and was killed by a falling tree in Washington; and Bennie Hanson, who was severely wounded in France. The officers for 1918 were Ole Larson as president; J. W. Johnson, Secretary; and Emily Johnson, Treasurer. Up until the Fires the club members were noted to be active in war work. As was noted however, "On the 12th of October of this year the great forest fire swept this and surrounding communities destroying buildings, equipment, and livestock. The club members and their neighbors lost practically all they had. Some members of the club were badly burned in the fire and some later died of their injuries. The clubhouse was burned but thanks to our faithful secretary, M. J. W. Johnson, the fire insurance

---

174 "Old, Lame and Gray, Refugee Horse Waits for His Master," *Duluth News Tribune,* May 27, 1919. Online at GenealogyBank.com. http://www.genealogybank.com/doc/newspapers/image.
175 "Dogs Stick to Thresholds; Perish While on Duty," *Duluth News Tribune,* October 23, 1918. Online at GenealogyBank.com. http://www.genealogybank.com/doc/newspapers/image.
176 "Hermantown Fire Refuge Sold by County for $500," *Duluth News Tribune,* August 13, 1919. Online at GenealogyBank.com. http://www.genealogybank.com/doc/newspapers/image.
177 Unpublished paper entitled, "History of Jackson Farmer's Club," in files of Hermantown Historical Society's History Center.

policies had been renewed just a short time before the fire. This insurance money together with the help from the government enabled us to go forward with new building plans. The courage and strength of our people was shown by the fact that practically every one returned to the land, and with faith in the future, began to rebuild in the ashes of destruction. The great news, coming about a month after the fire, that the war was over, gave heart to a stricken community. The boys who survived would now be coming home . . . In the spring of 1919 the club purchased a portable sawmill from the Relief Commission and in August they started sawing burned over timber for the members and neighbors. This mill was operated until 1922. . ." [178]

The First Agricultural Exposition after the 1918 Fires at the Jackson Club depicted. The photo was supplied courtesy of the Hermantown Historical Society, with special thanks to Bette Grussendorf and Delaine Carlson.

The Jackson Farmer's Club resumed holding its annual fall festival on September 15th and 16th of 1920, two years after the Fires. The photo shown above of the Jackson Club Festival after the 1918 Fire may be from this festival.

The 1920 fall festival was to be held at the Jackson School on a Wednesday and a Thursday. The farmers of the district

178 Unpublished paper entitled, "History of Jackson Farmers' Club," in files of Hermantown Historical Society's History Center.

". . . declare they have entirely recovered from the effects of the fires, and have decided to make the festival an annual affair in the future." [179] There was a program prepared by a committee headed by B. C. Erickson, which included farm talks by agriculturists, music, dancing, and games. Displays included exhibits of fruit and root crops, flowers, farm animals, and poultry.

Not be outdone by the Jackson Farmer's Club, the Hermantown Farmer's Club was going to host a similar festival on the 22nd and 23rd of September of 1920, Chairman C. G. Velander announced.

The entire countryside looked entirely different. As Kathryn Adams and Mary Schrock state in their book about Canosia Township and Pike Lake, "Returning settlers found few familiar landmarks to guide them along the roads. For some all that remained was twisted metal and a chimney. One man described wistfully all the fine furniture in his burned home and said, 'We will never have that much again.'"[180]

Edward Barr, of the Duluth News Tribune, described how life had been in the six months since the great fires of October 12, 1918. Some of the refugees spent the winter with family and friends in their cities and communities, while they tried to get back on their feet. But others, especially the farmers and settlers, went back to the ruins of their farms, and spent the winter on their homesteads in temporary buildings. Poignantly, the article said the people ". . . will soon plant evergreens above the graves of their dead. Most of the neat farm homes are gone, the fire's strange fancy perhaps leaving only the shrubbery along the stone foundation. In their places are the 'relief type' shacks furnished under the stress of haste and necessity by the Northern Minnesota Fire Relief Commission. These are seen by the hundreds. Many of them are empty." However, even though people rebuilt as quickly as possible and tried to put a brave face on it all, things would never be the same. The phrase, "Things would never be the same," was an often repeated sentiment voiced by the survivors.

---

179 "Fall Festival to Be Resumed. Farmers to Display Fruits and Crops for First Time since 1918 Forest Fires," *Duluth News Tribune*, September 11, 1920, Online at GenealogyBank.com. http://www.genealogybank.com/doc/newspapers/image.
180 Kathryn Adams and Mary Schrock, *Op. cit.*, p. 56.

# Part Two: MEMOIRS OF LOCAL RESIDENTS OR INFORMATION ABOUT THEM

## Introductory Remarks to Memoirs

As stated in the Preface, the following section is written in first person, a departure from the first part of the book. I have personal connections with most of these people or their family members through my own ancestors and founders of the community: August and Emilie Kohlts.

It contains the memoirs of the survivors, as well as accounts told by their descendants and information taken from newspaper stories of the day when direct stories were not available. I have also tried to tell something about the survivors and casualties, in an effort to bring a more human face to their stories, 100 years after their horrific experiences.

As I read through the listing of people who were known to have been killed by the Fires, I discovered surnames that were unfamiliar, such as the Lawyer family. The entire family perished in the Fires, leaving no area descendants to carry on the name.

A few people who were initially thought to have been from Hermantown, actually hailed from other nearby areas. Research indicated the Whittles family actually lived in Canosia Township, close to the Hermantown border. Lucinda Jordan was another such person. She also resided in Canosia Township, and apparently worked for a wealthy family who had a summer home on Pike Lake. One family group killed was listed as the "Falitier" family of Adolph. "Falitier" was probably a misspelling for the surname of Pelletier. Two young children, Violet and Edward Archambeau, were from Duluth. However, all of these people were very close to the Hermantown township official borders.

Although these accounts center on the Hermantown area, there are also stories of people from bordering areas. In 1918 boundaries between townships, villages, and cities were not sharply defined. The stories of people in the proximity of Hermantown were very similar as they attempted to survive the Fires.

### Louis Archambault
**(November 15, 1828 to October 12, 1918)**

I was surprised to learn that my great-great grandfather, Louis Archambault, perished in the 1918 Forest Fire. A grandson of one of Louis' daughters (Emma Archambault Becotte), named Brian Becotte, was kind enough to send me a copy of a death certificate as well as the article from the Duluth newspaper.

"Louis Archambeault, who perished at his home in Hermantown, in Saturday night's fire, was a pioneer of Duluth. He came to this city 40 years ago [*1878]*. He was 90 years old. Three sons, Amedi, Felix *[my great-grandfather*] and Edmond, all of Duluth, and four daughters, Mrs. C. Becotte, Duluth, Mrs. Jerry Pelletier, of Adolph, Mrs.

A. Boire of Duluth and Mrs. Fred Krause of Duluth survive him. He had 26 grandchildren and 10 great grandchildren."[181] His name was listed in the Known Dead, with his body having been taken the Olson and Hoppanyan Mortuary.[182]

According to his Probate Court file, at the time of his death he had $200.00 in cash, as well as 39 and ½ half acres of real estate worth $800.00 near Duluth. Twenty acres were termed "unimproved lands," and the homestead occupied 19 ½ acres.[183] This was filed in St. Louis County Probate Court on November 14, 1941, file #12163, many years after his demise. *(See Addendum IV for a retyped copy of the Wrongful Death Order.)*

The Inventory from that same file lists, beside the real estate, the following other personal property: "Claim against the United States Government for the wrongful death of descendent arising out of the October 12, 1918 Forest Fire in the sum of $200.00, of which there has been paid 40% of $200.00, leaving a balance of $120.00."

*(Written August 21, 2013, by Connie Jacobson.)*

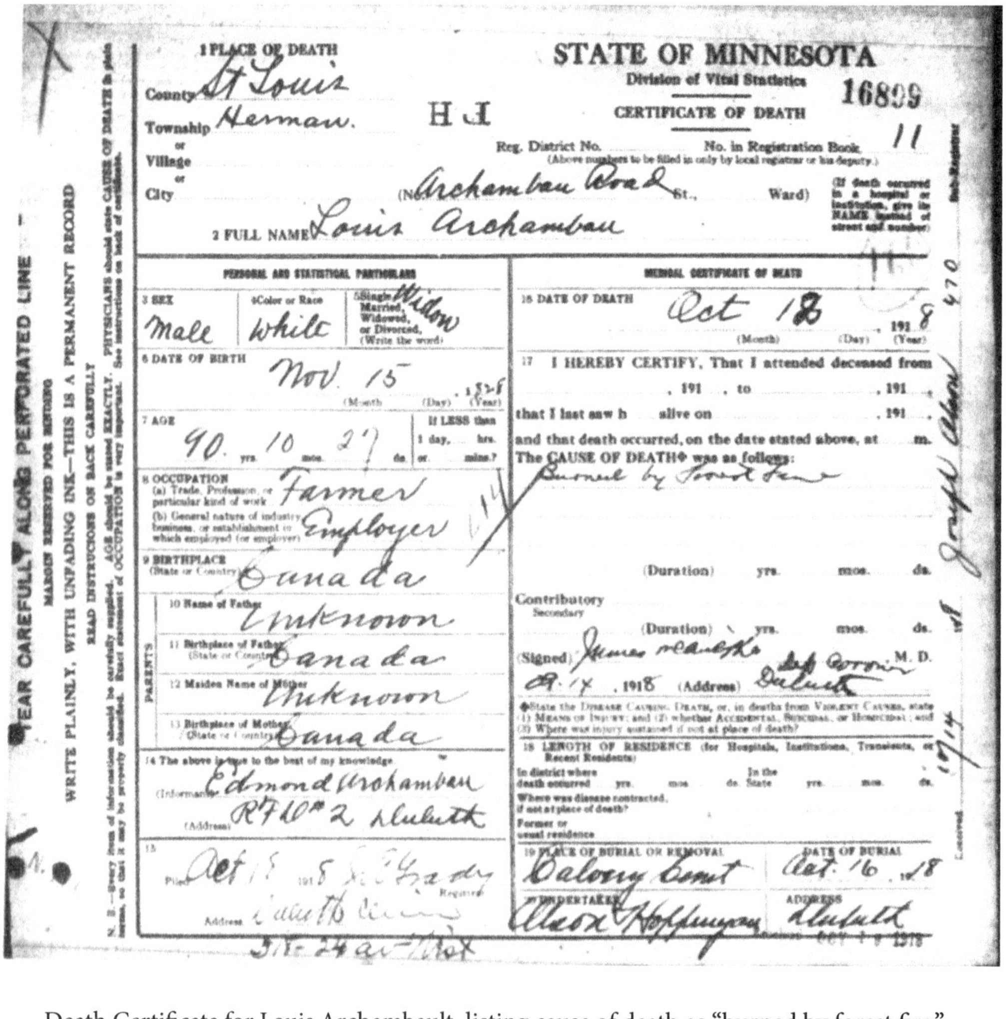

STATE OF MINNESOTA
Division of Vital Statistics
CERTIFICATE OF DEATH
16809

1 PLACE OF DEATH
County St Louis
Township Herman
Reg. District No. No. in Registration Book 11
City (No. Archambau Road St., Ward)
2 FULL NAME Louis Archambau

PERSONAL AND STATISTICAL PARTICULARS
3 SEX Male
4 Color or Race White
5 Single, Married, Widowed, or Divorced Widow
6 DATE OF BIRTH Nov. 15
7 AGE 90 yrs. 10 mos. 27 ds.
8 OCCUPATION Farmer
(b) General nature of industry Employer
9 BIRTHPLACE Canada
10 Name of Father Unknown
11 Birthplace of Father Canada
12 Maiden Name of Mother Unknown
13 Birthplace of Mother Canada
14 The above is true to the best of my knowledge
(Informant) Edmond Archambau
(Address) RFD #2 Duluth
15 Filed Oct 1 1918

MEDICAL CERTIFICATE OF DEATH
16 DATE OF DEATH Oct 12 1918
17 I HEREBY CERTIFY, That I attended deceased from , 191 , to , 191
that I last saw h alive on , 191
and that death occurred, on the date stated above, at m.
The CAUSE OF DEATH was as follows:
Burned by forest fire
(Signed) M. D.
, 1918 (Address) Duluth
18 LENGTH OF RESIDENCE
19 PLACE OF BURIAL OR REMOVAL Calvary Cemt
DATE OF BURIAL Oct. 16, 18
20 UNDERTAKER Olson Hoppanyan
ADDRESS Duluth

Death Certificate for Louis Archambault, listing cause of death as "burned by forest fire."

181 "Finds Wife and Child in Ruins of Their Home. Many Pitiful Tales of Lost Members of Families Disclosed as Death Toll Grows. Pioneer Perishes," *Duluth News Tribune,* October 15, 1918. Online at GenealogyBank.com. http://www.genealogybank.com/gbnk/newspapers/doc

182 "Known Dead-Duluth List," *Duluth News Tribune,* October 15, 1918. Online at GenealogyBank.com. http://www.genealogybank.com/gbnk/newspapers/doc.

183 St. Louis County Probate Court file #12163, filed October 14, 1918. (On Microfilm at St. Louis County Courthouse in Duluth, MN, and retyped by author.)

## Mrs. Louis Archambeau and Infant

A woman and her baby died about a month later.

"Funeral Services for Mrs. Louis Archambeau, age 23, a refugee who died of influenza at the Moose Hall Friday night, were held yesterday afternoon. Her infant child died yesterday morning. Mr. and Mrs. Archambeau, whose home at Hermantown was destroyed, have been making their home at 707 North Twentieth Avenue West." [184]

## Cyril and Alvina Archambeau

In 1989 the eleventh child of Cyril (11-15-1875 to ?) and Alvina Archambeau (1879 to 12-26-1936), Ruby (Archambeau) LaRoque (10-14-1917 to 12-30-2009) wrote some information for her family. She refers to the 1918 Fires.

*(Brother Raymond) said his earliest recollection was the log house the family lived in. This house was located on the corner of what's now known as Piedmont and Hutchinson Road. I don't have any idea how long they lived there. My father then bought another house in the same area from Carl Olson. At that time my mother had eleven children.*

*October 12, 1918, was a day of disaster for our family and most of the people in the Hermantown and Piedmont area. The weather was tinder dry and the winds were hot and blowing very hard. There were seven children at home ranging in age from one year to seventeen years and my mother. She had a very sick little boy to care for. Our brother, Edward, who had broken his arm and had a bad infection in it, was very sick. Can you imagine how all hell broke loose when the fire came upon them? Everyone was running for their lives.*

*Maybe a lot of you who will read this will remember of hearing about the 1918 Forest Fire on October 12th.*

*There was one man in the neighborhood who had a truck and was trying to help the people. His name was Dan Donaghey. Three little girls were in this truck, two of the Gray children and our sister Violet and many more. So many people were hanging on to the truck that he missed the road and the truck went down a deep embankment on the Hutchinson Road and burst into flames. The older people got away but the three small children burned to death in the truck. (Violet died in the fire of 1918. Edward died from smoke from the 1918 fire.)*

*The older members of our family were in town working. The Home Guards and the police were on duty to receive the people coming into town. No one was allowed to go up the hill. Our sister, Delia, carried me (Ruby). She said she couldn't count the times her feet left the road and she would fall in the ditch, crawl up on the road and start running again. The wind was so strong and the night was black as pitch from the smoke.*

*The Home Guards met some of the people and found places for them to stay. Evelyn was only seven. I don't know who was taking care of her. She was taken to the hospital and hospitalized. All of her hair had to be cut off and her face was burned very badly. Brother Clifford's ears were burned and also his face and hands. A total stranger to our family took me home to her house. Her name was Mrs. LaBuddy. Delia had to find me and take me home. Louise, we believe, was also on the truck and placed in a stranger's home after the accident. She was twelve years old and it was several days before she was found and returned to the family.*

*After the fire our father found a place to live. We were then living on 27th Avenue West and 3rd Street in Duluth. Alice said that's where she was born. No wonder, as time went by, my mother had a nervous breakdown after my brother, Bobby was born.*

*We lived at 27th and 3rd Street for about two years before moving back to Hermantown.* [185]

---

184 "Hermantown Refugee is Dead; Infant Precedes Her," Duluth *News Tribune,* November 17, 1918. Online at GenealogyBank.com. http://www.genealogybank.com/gbnk/newspapers/doc.

185 Ruby (Archambeau) LaRoque, unpublished Archambeau family history book, 1989, a copy of which is retained at the Hermantown History Center.

## Ken Archambeau

Ken Archambeau shared his experience with Bette Grussendorf in 2008, which was included in an article in the *Hermantown Star* from October of that year.

"Kenny Archambeau shared his experience that took place on his grandparent's family farm, which was located by Haines Road and Morris Thomas Road. When the fire was approaching, the family, in a hurry, tried to get all members into the root cellar. As this occurred, in came a deer! The deer went into a corner and stayed until the door opened and then bolted out at first light."

## Roy Bang

### (May 23, 1903 to July 31, 1985)

Although Roy and his family lived in nearby Solway Township in 1918, in later years he lived in Hermantown on the Lindahl Road. His detailed memories of the Fires in an adjoining area are included to give another view into the experiences of people during those harrowing hours and days.

The following article was included in a magazine entitled, *Trackin' Back Magazine*, Vol. 3.The copy of the article retained by the Hermantown History Center had the fourth digit of the magazine's year obscured. Therefore, I was unable to determine the exact year, but knew it was sometime during 1980, 1981, 1982, 1983, 1984, or even 1985, since Roy died July 31, 1985. [Cjj, 1-24-2017]

The article was titled, "1918 Fire Remembered," unlisted author/interviewer.

*Roy Bang was nearly killed during the 1918 Fire. . . .*

*"I was five years old when we moved out there* (to the farm) *in 1909. . . And the next year I started school in a little one-room school where the teacher taught eight grades. . . I graduated one year early. I skipped the third grade. Maybe that's what's been wrong with me ever since I skipped the third grade!*

*Then I worked, there was no high school. Then I worked on the farm until 1918. That was the forest fire. I was 15.*

*Now right there is something to remember. My whole face and hands were burnt. I had third degree burns on my hands and first degree on my face.*

*I remember the afternoon of the fire. Part of the fire had already swept past our house and we were out fighting the fire behind the barn. It was getting towards four-thirty . . . because my mother had been to West Duluth and she had come up on the train and she got home before our place burnt down. So actually our place probably didn't burn until about five.*

*We thought for a while it was going to miss our place and we had one of the neighbor's horses over there and they had moved some of their stuff which was laying out in our yard.*

*So we were there and my dad and I and one of the neighbors were fighting the fire in the back . . . Then all of a sudden it seemed like the wind switched and the fire came right down towards us. We had put all our stock in the barn so they wouldn't be in the way for us while were fighting the fire. So we beat it to the barn to try and let the cattle out of the barn if we possibly could. Well, my dad and I went in.*

*We had threshed oats maybe two weeks prior to the fire . . . You could see there was a little bit of fire starting up in the top of the straw stack in the* (barn's) *driveway.*

*We went into the horse barn. . . . The horses were tied with a slip knot so we wasted no time getting them out and I backed out. . .I opened the door to go out with the horses and the door was one solid sheet of flame. . .That's how quickly it went and that was the only way we could get out.*

*I quickly shut the door and told my dad (he was right behind me with the other horses) that the door was all afire. So we put the horses back in their stalls and we both got together and I opened the door.*

*I got outside and my dad followed me. But you see, I was fortunate . . . because I was wearing a wool flannel shirt and of course it didn't catch fire as fast. I had my hands up to cover my face.*

*But my dad was wearing a cotton chambray shirt and this caught fire so his clothes were on fire . . . and he ran to the toilet to try and get the fire off. The house was 100-150 feet away from the barn and he came out of there (the toilet) and he was still burning. He came dashing up to the house . . . I met him with a pail of water and I threw the pail of water on him when he came in. And, you know, this involved not over five minutes of time – from the time we came out of the barn and were in the house. . . .*

*My dad went upstairs to get whatever legal papers . . . and whatever money he had. He came down and went and opened the back door and the flames from the barn came and hit the back door. That's how quickly everything went. We shut the door and had to go out the front way.*

*Mother came from downtown that day and all she did was grab a rug from off the floor and threw it around dad. I picked up a mackinaw that belonged to my brother who was in the Navy at the time and threw that around me, and I went down the road.*

*And you couldn't see because it was so dark and smoky. So the three of us went down together and got to the corner of the Maple Grove and Munger Shaw Roads* (where the Munger School used to be). *Right in that corner there was a potato field and I was 10-15 feet in front of my folks and I turned and went down the Munger Shaw Road, never realizing they went down to the potato field. So that's where we got separated. I headed on towards Munger. I got about half way down where the ballfield is now and there was one solid sheet of flame.* (He continued to look for his parents but could not find them.) *So I didn't know what to do.*

*Then I happened to think that the Canadian National comes through there just east of there and I know there was a culvert just under the railroad track. It was a timber culvert but it was all covered up with dirt on the west side and this is where I crawled in.*

*And there's where I stayed until about 11 o'clock at night. It seemed like everything had died down by then. But in the meantime I didn't know what to do. So I kind of rolled over, managed to get a jack knife out of my pocket, and dug a hole in the sand in the bottom of this culvert, because my hands were just like they were on fire. And then I put my hands in there and I shoved dirt over the top of them with my forehead.*

*Then about 11 o'clock there was a house maybe a block away that hadn't burned. . . . So I went up to the house and there was nobody there. I tried to get into the house, but the condition of my hands—I couldn't open the door which made me think the house was locked. So I picked a clothes pole out in the yard and I broke the window and crawled in through the window. Well, I didn't dare sleep in the bed for fear of fire, so I dragged some bedclothes out and laid them on the ground.*

*Now this is the peculiar part of it. I have to laugh when I think of this now. There was a pig and eight little ones out there. She was running out there . . . . When I tried to roll myself up in the quilts and stuff the pig and the littles ones all tried to crawl in there with me. I have to laugh every time I think of this, you know.*

*And there was a sink tub full of water and I'd get up periodically and dip my hands in this to try and get the fire out . . . . It must have been three or four in the morning before I finally fell asleep . . . . Well, I slept until about eight or eight-thirty and I got up and saw this other house that had not burned, there by the school. And that had not burned either.*

*So I got up and walked down there and went over and knocked on the door. Mrs. Sola answered the door . . . . She didn't know who I was because my face and hands were so swollen up. So I told her who I was and asked her if she had seen my dad and mother. And she said, "Where are you going?" And I said I was going to walk back home and see if they were up there. And she said, "You're not going anywhere. You're going to the hospital." So she called Gus Larson and told him to take me to the hospital. The train would be at the depot at about 9:30, so that's how I wound up in St. Mary's Hospital for six weeks.*

*My dad was the last man to leave St. Mary's Hospital. He didn't get out of there until March, 1919. He was badly burned. Now his face looked more like my hands used to — that hard, shiny look. And he could only open his hands about so far.*

*So we lived in West Duluth up until the first of May, 1919. . . . There was a little place right near ours that didn't burn. It had two rooms in it. So we moved in there. In the meantime we had gotten a team of horses and some equipment from the Red Cross and we started to do our spring planting . . . . But we lost everything (to the fire.) The only thing that was left was a cat and her feet were burnt. Otherwise, the rest of it was all gone.*

*In 1933 my brother and I still weren't working . . . and he said to me, "What do you say we rent the old Taylor's place and we gamble on potatoes?". . . . And from that time until 1937 we rented the place and raised potatoes. We didn't do too badly.* [186]

## Frank Henry Berglund
## (June 11, 1916 to October 13, 1918)

In a listing of fatalities of the report of the National Guard was a "Baby Berglund," of Hermantown, the Maple Grove Road, and two years old. His baptism occurred March 4, 1917, at Zion Lutheran Church. He died on the 13th of October at St. Luke's Hospital, was listed as being at the Fred Olson Mortuary, and was subsequently buried at Bethany Cemetery on the Morris Thomas Road. His father was Carl Berglund; his mother, Freda Johnson Berglund.

## The Thomas and Martha Berntsen Family

David Peterson interviewed and taped Raymond Berntsen's story about his family's experiences during the 1918 Fires. In turn, Sue (Berntsen) Swanstrom listened to the taped interview and put their experiences into writing. Thomas Berntsen was born on March 18, 1887, in Egersund, Norway, according to his World War I Registration card, and died January 2, 1974. His wife, Martha Pauline Pederson, was born November 1, 1892, and passed away April 24, 1986. Raymond Edward Berntsen, their eldest surviving child, was born July 11, 1913, and died April 21, 2009. Another son, Walter Berntsen, was born February 14, 1915, and died April 18, 2002. In a photo taken in the spring of 1918 at the ditch camp where Tom was a supervisor and Martha was the camp cook, the family is depicted. Tom had lost his arm from a sawmill accident in 1917; baby Stanley, held by his mother Martha, reportedly died from the flu epidemic shortly after the photo was taken. The story was given by Roger Berntsen, a member of the Hermantown Historical Society and a son of Walter Berntsen, to Bob Swanstrom of the Hermantown Historical Society late in 2017.

### A Miracle

*Martha woke early; she had chores to do. She had the daily washing, cooking, and bread to bake, she had two young sons, Raymond and Walter to tend to, and she was eight months pregnant. She also had to cook at the ditch camp where her husband Tom was supervisor, a job he began ten months before.*

*The day passed quickly and Martha was cooking dinner when she heard a loud ruckus in the front yard. She saw the neighbor running toward the house, her arms waving, shouting, "My house is burning, my house is burning, someone please help!" Immediately Tom was off to help. He thought Martha and the boys would be safe at the house. No one then knew the extent of what became known as the largest natural disaster in Minnesota History.*

*Martha was worried. There was a drought the past two years, and last summer was the worst. It was so dry everyone*

186"1918 Fire Remembered," *Trackin' Back Magazine,* unlisted author/interviewer, Vol. 3, May'8?. The copy retained at the Hermantown History Center had part of the last digit of the year obscured, and all I know for certain is that it was from 1981, 1982, or even 1983, several months prior to his passing.

*feared the threat of fire. The neighbors discussed with Tom and Martha over the dry months, their plans to survive the flames if the fires came. One neighbor thought they would place their family of ten in the root cellar. They claimed they would be snug as bugs in a rug. The flames would burn the tall grass over the cellar but inside the root cellar they would survive. Another neighbor, Sara and her husband, planned on climbing down the water well where next to the cool water they would be safe. In fact they imagined looking up to watch as the flames passed over. Another neighbor said they were the luckiest of all. They prepared a boat down on the shore of the lake and if the flames came their family would run across the hot dry field, jump into the boat, paddle to the middle where they would be safe from the fire. After all, water and flames don't mix.*

*Martha was trying to decide what she and the boys would do if the fires came their way. Suddenly she heard another loud ruckus in the front yard. She looked out and saw Tom running, arms waving and yelling, "Come Martha, it's not safe here anymore! The fire's coming! It's time to leave!" Martha was unprepared; she wanted to get some belongings from the house but Tom wouldn't let her. "There's no time!" he yelled, so they escaped with only the clothes on their backs. He managed to get them to the Martin Road where Tom said, "Martha, you and the boys wait here. Someone will come along and give you a ride to the work farm." He kissed her good bye, and before Martha could argue with him, he was running down the road to help fight the fires. Alone and scared Martha waited with her boys. The wind had picked up; it was blowing hard and the smell of smoke was stronger. Soon a stranger came and offered the three of them a ride to the work farm.*

*At the work farm Martha noticed an Army truck parked by the main building. The driver told her he was going to Duluth and anyone who wanted a ride could join him. Martha loaded her two small boys into the bed of the truck, and then shimmied up next to them. She noticed two woolen blankets and a bucket of water in the corner of the truck. She moved the boys next to the cab and told them that if the flames came they were to lie down and she would cover them with the blanket and use the water to keep them wet so the flames wouldn't burn them. Suddenly the winds were blowing at hurricane force, rocking the truck. The smoke was blinding. Martha could barely see and her eyes were stinging. She looked to the horizon and saw the sky turning black. She knew something was about to happen and yelled for the boys to get down. Yet, the boys were curious, they peeked over the side of the truck toward the horizon and they watched in fear as the black sky turned amber red. Martha yelled, "Get down, boys, get down!" She threw the blanket over their tiny heads and doused them with water. As she looked up she saw the piney forest explode into flames. Every direction she looked there were flames. Overhead appeared sheets of flames and balls of fire tumbling out of the smoky amber skies. The smoke made it hard for her to breathe; the unborn baby in her belly felt like a ton of bricks. She fell to her knees and crawled next to her boys and pulled a corner of the wet wool blanket up over her face. She thought of Tom and her neighbors, and heard her young son Raymond cry, "Are we moving yet, Mom? Are we moving?" Then all went black.*

*Martha woke. She's not sure what time it was or how long she was out, but she knew she was okay and that her boys were alive. She glanced at the burn marks left on her skirt and on the boys' blanket and realized how close they came to certain death. Then she peered over the edge of the truck and saw the main building of the work farm where the truck had been parked the night before, and realized they hadn't moved at all! She looked beyond the main building and saw the piney forest burnt to the ground. All that was left were smoldering tree stumps. The flames came right up to them and continued towards Duluth. They had been in the middle of a burning inferno, yet they were still alive! A miracle!*

*The next two days were chaos with relatives and neighbors stumbling about trying to find their loved ones. Two days later Tom found Martha and the boys. They hugged and kissed, finding it hard to believe the four of them made it through the fire alive!*

*Tom told Martha his story of survival. "While fighting the fire with other volunteers at the neighbor's house, we realized that the fire was beyond control," he recalled, "As the flames approached we all jumped into the neighbor's Model-T and fled towards Duluth." The smoke was so thick, two men, one on each side, lay on the running boards and ran their fingers along the gravel in the road, shouting to the driver to veer one way or another, so they wouldn't end up in the ditch. As they contin-*

*ued toward Duluth they stopped to pick up men along the road. By the time they got to town thirteen men were clinging to the sides of the car. They made it through the flames and smoke and were the last to make it to Duluth. A few minutes later they all would have perished in the flames.*

*He told her the sad truth about the neighbors. Remember the family in the root cellar? They all suffocated. Sara and her husband, the couple that shimmied down the water well, both died from suffocation. The other neighbor with the boat: they crossed the hot dry field that night, jumped into the boat, and paddled to the middle of the lake but the winds were so strong that it capsized their boat and they drowned.*

*Hundreds lost their lives; thousands lost everything except the clothes on their backs. And all on one hot, dry, black, and smoky October night.*

*Days passed and a month later Martha gave birth to a happy and healthy baby girl they named Eleanor. Over the next several years, with the help of the Salvation Army, they and their neighbors rebuilt their lives, homes, and their farms.*

*Years later Martha heard a ruckus in the front yard. She looked out the window to see the beautiful Minnesota sky and watched her children play in the cool green grass. She looked to the horizon and thought back to the night of the horrific October fires. She smiled and thought how lucky they were to have made it through the 1918 Fires of Northern Minnesota. But for the chance of fate that split the flames as they approached the work farm and the old army truck, Martha, Raymond, Walter and all of their descendants (all of us) would not be here to celebrate life.*

*Life truly is a miracle.*

## Otto and Bertha Pauline (Kohlts) (nickname of Lena) Busch

**(Otto-May 6, 1862 to June 2, 1944; Bertha-February 16, 1864 to November 8, 1933)**

Their house burned, and they stayed for a time with Frank and Frieda Kohlts in Duluth, where the Kohlts family had moved about ten years earlier. When they returned to the farm to retrieve whatever they could from the root cellar, fifteen year old Bill Kohlts remarked he would be glad when the potatoes were gone because they tasted like smoke. [187]

## Art Carlson

Art Carlson had a few vivid memories of the Fire.

*"The wind reached 75 miles an hour," according to Art Carlson, "and it was raining sparks, I remember. I was out milking when I heard wagons at a dead gallop on the road in front of the house. They were crammed with people, heading for town. I chased the cows into the field and got into town." Another family hiding in a root cellar was forced out by the wind that was throwing pieces of burning wood through the rear opening. They sought shelter under a rock pile and survived.*[188]

## Mr. Albert Dahl, Mary Dahl, and sons Ingwall and Calvin

**(Albert born 1870; Mary, born 1874; Ingwall, 1895; Calvin, 1901)**

*The Journal News*, the newspaper of Two Harbors, reported that the Dahls, farmers on the Hermantown Road out of Duluth, lost their farm. They themselves narrowly escaped the Fires with their lives. Mrs. Dahl was a sister of John P. Sande of Two Harbors. Other than that, no other information is given about the Dahl family. [189]

---

187 William Kohlts, E-mail message to author, October 23, 2013.
188 Anne Stultz Bailey,"Wind and Fire, an October Holocaust!" *Duluth Budgeteer Special Edition*, July 18, 1979.
189 Carol Illikainen, *Firebeast: The Fires of 1918*, p. 18, published by Moose Lake Area Historical Society in 1994, and republished with corrections and additions, 2016.

## The Alfred and Alice Erickson Family

This tragic tale is a combination of my own memories of conversations between my parents, Helmer (1913 – 2006) and Evelyn (1917 – 2005) Jacobson, and Bertil (1913 – 2001) and Esther Erickson, supplemented by the memories as related by Dora Erickson Krueger and Bertil Erickson.

My father's childhood friend, Bertil Erickson, vividly remembered literally running for his life to the east on what today is the area of the Hagberg Road west of Midway Road, toward the Midway Road. The 40 acre family farm was located on what today is the western end of the Hagberg Road, which was at that time more of a driveway than an actual road. Bertil was the oldest child of Alfred and Alice Erickson at 5 years of age; Dora (Krueger) was 3; and little Marie Charlotta was 17 months old, having been born on March 22, 1917. [*Note by author: Her middle name is given as Charlotte and Charlotta.*] What's more, mother Alice was expecting another child in 4 months. His father, Alfred, had left for work, riding on his bicycle, to the old work farm located where the minimum security prison camp is today.

There was a lot of choking smoke, and the sky was red to the west as the rising winds blew sparks around them. As Bertil told Brady Bergeson in 1995, "The sky was real smoky and the sun was like a ball of fire in the west."[190] Bertil remembered that his mother ". . . had tried to get her belongings out with a shawl she filled up."[191] The family stumbled as fast as they could through the uneven and rough ground of a dry swamp, and remembered panicking when a large haystack that was on fire landed beside them. They scrambled through a barbed wire fence, and Bertil's shoe got caught on it. It had to be left there so he had to run the rest of the way with one shoe. Before they reached the Midway Road their hair was singed from the sparks raining down around them. Seeing their plight, a neighbor came to help them. He carried little Marie on his back, and took her with him to his house, from which he hoped to save some valuables. While frantically searching through his house, he set little Marie down outside. When he came back to get her, the house was burning down.

By this time a car stopped and picked up Bertil, his mother, and little Dora to take them to Adolph for a train ride into the safety of Duluth. The neighbor, whose last name was Swenson, was going to meet them at Adolph, but neither he nor little Marie were anywhere to be seen. However, the family couldn't wait any longer, because fire was burning almost every boxcar on the track. They were hurriedly loaded into one of the boxcars that wasn't burning, and escaped to Duluth, where a very worried Alfred met them at the Armory. For two long nights they slept on the floor with many other people crowded in like sardines.

The day after the fire Alfred left to see what had happened to Marie as well as the neighbor who had offered to care for little Marie Charlotte. Alfred walked all the way from the Armory, on the shores of Lake Superior, up the old Miller Trunk Highway, to Four Corners, seeing many dead and burned bodies along the way, and proceeded south on Midway Road, and then toward the family's homestead west of the Midway Road.

There Swenson met him and delivered both the good and the bad news: the Erickson's house was still standing, but Marie had perished in the fire. Although the house survived, it was slightly damaged. However, the brand new barn, pump house, shed, and two wooden barrels each holding 55 gallons of water burned. All their cattle had burned to death except for one badly burned cow in the cabbage patch, which had to be put down. Swenson said the flames were so intense he couldn't get to the place he had set Marie Charlotta outside his house, which had been consumed by fire. Poor Alice was haunted by this terrible tragedy all of her life.

---

190 Brady Bergeson, Interview with Bertil Erickson, *Hermantown Star*, October 5, 1995.
191 *Ibid.*
[11] Moose Lake Area Historical Society, *1918 Fire Stories: A Collection of Stories and Documents Related to the Forest Fires of 1918 that Devastated a Large Area of Northeastern Minnesota*, p. 37, printed by Paper Hog, Duluth, MN, 2003.

Bertil Erickson remembered that his mother's shawl was sitting in the house, untouched by the fire. His father had a substantial amount of money hidden in the house, which was still intact.[192] An uncle who lived on the same road as the Alfred Erickson family saved himself by jumping into a well.

Except for the loss of his baby sister, Bertil felt his family was lucky to have survived ". . . what many survivors called 'hell on earth.'" He also recalled the headline of the Duluth News Tribune in 1968, on the fiftieth anniversary of the Fire. It was, "The Day the Sun Died." [193]

The funeral for Marie Charlotta Erickson was announced in the newspaper. "The funeral of Mary, 18 month old daughter of Alfred Erickson of Hermantown, who perished in the flames, will be held at 1 o'clock this afternoon from the Bell Bros. Undertaking parlors, Rev. Christian Swenson, Pastor of Elim Lutheran Church officiating. Interment in the Hermantown* Cemetery."[194] [*Note by author; she was actually buried at the Bethany Cemetery, located in Hermantown on the Hermantown Road.]*

Memorial Marker for Maria Charlotta Erickson. From FindAGrave.com.

192 *Ibid.*
193 *Ibid.*
194 "Brief Private Funerals Held for Fire Dead. Numerous Interments in Duluth Given by Rushed Undertakers. Baby Burned," *Duluth News Tribune,* October 17, 1918. Online at GenealogyBank.com. http://www.genealogy bank.com/gbnk/newspapers/doc.

## Arthur Fichtner (1894 to 1974) and Clara Fichtner

Local Hermantown historian, Arthur Fichtner, included his memories of the fire in an article he wrote about the family farm upon which he grew up.

*"On May 12, 1918, my Dad, Theodore Fichtner, died after a long illness and on October 12th of the same year the big forest fire swept the place clean. We had been to market that day. At this time Albert Busch Sr. (1903 to 1989) was working for us and he would start for the market about five in the morning with the team and I would do the chores and follow an hour later with the car. When we got word that there was fire in some slashing across from our place Mother (Rosa Kohlts Fichtner – November 28, 1867 to June 15, 1938) and I rushed home with the car. Albert was to clean up at the market and follow but by the time he got to the Haines Road the National Guard was stationed along the roads and would not let anybody out of town. Mrs. Sundell was in town with her horse and buggy and she was also trapped and could not get home. When the fire got so bad that we could do nothing more we decided to try to get into town.*

*In the meantime Mr. Sundell, who had no means of transportation at home, came across our field with two year old Henry Sundell (1915 – 1982) on one arm, a sack with his personal belongings over his shoulder and two little girls hanging onto his coattails. We piled them, my mother, me, and Uncle Henry, who had come to help, into the car and started out. The headlights were no better than candles, and several times almost ran into horses and cattle on the road.*

*We got into Town without further incident and the next morning when I got back the fire had burned anything that would burn and the wind had even swept the ashes away.*

*We had threshed about 400 bushels of oats a few days before which was piled on the feed floor and was popping like popcorn all that day.*

*The cattle we found in the back pasture where the lead cow had been killed by a falling tree and the rest were all standing around her.*

*In 1915 Uncle Henry and I took the old timber hay barns apart and with our wood sawing outfit rigged like a sawmill we ripped all the timber into studs and built a hay barn, on the old foundation."* [195]

In an e-mail dated October 23, 2013, to the author from a descendant, William Kohlts, the following information was relayed.

"The Fichtner farm on the Maple Grove Road burned. A small house was built with plans and materials donated by the Red Cross after the Fire, which was still on the property as of the 1980s. The main house was later rebuilt on the foundation of the one that was lost."

One of Clara and Art Fichtner's grand nieces, Patricia Gregory, also had memories of the Fichtner farm. In a letter to Nancy Hanson, on file at the Northeast Minnesota Historical Center, she wrote about remembering seeing the stark landscape and burned surroundings of the farmstead. She wrote that the Fichtner family rebuilt and used their Red Cross 'shack' as either a summer kitchen or a chicken coop thereafter. From 1946 to 1970 she visited the farm several times to visit her great Aunt Clara and Great Uncle Art Fichtner while they were living there. [196]

Clara Fichtner also had memories of the fire and its aftermath.

*It was with a mixture of good humor and determination that the people of Hermantown began the long process of rebuilding after the holocaust. New homes, churches and schools would be built. The Red Cross provided some supplies as well*

---

195 Arthur Fichtner, "The History of the Fichtner Farm: A Reference for My Grandsons," November, 1973, unpublished manuscript on file at the Hermantown Historical Center.

196 Patricia Gregory Reminiscence of 1918 Fire, (handwritten letter to Nancy Hanson dated December 19, 2003), on file at the Northeast Minnesota Historical Collections, Archives and Special Collections, Kathryn A. Martin Library, Room 202, University of Minnesota Duluth, 416 Library Drive, Duluth, MN 55812-3001. (S6072)

*as lumber for a 12 x 16 building as temporary replacement for each lost home. The Red Cross lumber is still in part of the Stebner living room, and is what Clara Fichtner calls her "summer kitchen." For three years after the fire, the Jackson Farmer's Club served the community rebuilding efforts with the use of its sawmill, for sawing burned timber into lumber. The Club began a purchasing association to replace destroyed farm machinery, later known as the Farmer's Exchange. Community barns were built to take care of the surviving cattle, and the following spring, planting would begin. "You just started over," said Clara Fichtner, "but it would never be the same."* [197]

## Oscar and Rosa Fichtner

**(Theodore Oscar Fichtner – August 18, 1860 to May 12, 1918)**
**Rosalie Emilie Kohlts Fichtner – November 28, 1867 to June 15, 1938)**

Patricia Gregory wrote that the Oscar and Rosa Fichtner family farm was destroyed. Their daughter, Flora Fichtner (Mrs. Henry Klosowsky, August 19, 1890 to December 9, 1941), was Patricia's maternal grandmother. The area where the house had been was leveled before rebuilding, and the only thing from the farm was a lump of silver which had been Rosa's treasured silver service. Patricia remembered seeing a building that the Red Cross had set up for Oscar and Rosa to live in until their permanent house could be finished. [198]

## Peter Fishan

**(June, 1849 to November 29, 1926)**

Peter Fishan was one of the Hermantown residents who gave up farming after he was burned out and injured in the Fires. His homestead entry for 80 acres was issued in November of 1877, making him one of the early settlers in Hermantown. Peter Fishan was named to be an overseer of highways for road district number 1 at the annual township meeting of March 11, 1878. The following year he ran unsuccessfully for the position of a township supervisor. However, on March 1, 1880, he was elected both supervisor and constable, posts he held for at least several years. The Duluth Minnesota 1918 City Directory gave his address as R. F. D. 2, box 98, which was a Hermantown address, while on the other hand the 1926 Duluth City Directory listed his address as 416 North 11$^{th}$ Avenue West in Duluth. Being injured in the Fires, he was hospitalized and treated for his burns at St. Luke's Hospital in Duluth. His wife, Amelia Augusta Fritz, the daughter of another early Hermantown family, died on October 22, 1920, perhaps being weakened by the 1918 Fires. Peter and Amelia Fishan had three children who were grown to adulthood at the time of the Fires: Emma, Luisa, and John.

Wilmer (Bud) Wagner referred to the Fishan family in his memories of the Fires. "*. . . The Peter Fishan family just across the road from us was completely burned out so they sold the land and moved to Duluth. The cement floors of some of the buildings remained for years and I would go there and play with all the nails that were left from the fire. My dad bought thirty acres of this land and by the time he was through farming he had it all cleared out. A lot of the rocks had been dug and blasted out; small ones were picked and ditches dug for drainage. Also the concrete floors were removed to balance the rusty nails; many were square ones, and a lot of hay and mostly potatoes grown on it. One of the Fishan daughters used to come in the summer to buy pickling cucumbers from my folks.*"

---

197_Ann Stultz Bailey, "Wind and Fire, an October Holocaust!" *Duluth Budgeteer Special Edition,* July 13, 1979.
198 Patricia Gregory Op. cit.

## Alice Mathilda Gulbranson
### (1906 to December 25, 1918)

The daughter of Eric Gulbranson (January 17, 1877 to November 19, 1962) and Emma (Christensen) Gulbranson (May 27, 1888 to July 7, 1962), of Adolph, had a fire related death. According to a family tree of Per Gulbrandsson, provided to me by Delaine Carlson, the cause of death for 10 year old Alice was pneumonia, resulting from the Fire of 1918. Her funeral service was held December 30, 1918, and she is buried in the Hermantown Cemetery on the Morris Thomas Road. [199] (I don't know if this is one of the children referred to in the "Mrs. Gulbranson and Children" account following.)

## Mrs. Gulbranson and Children

The following paragraph was retyped by Lucille M. Pearson from a third extra edition of the Duluth News Tribune from October 13, 1918, and is included in her book on the history of Fredenberg.

"With firebrands falling from each side of the road threatening their clothing with fire, Mrs. Gulbranson and her eight children, the youngest of whom is only two weeks old, and two neighbor women, rode three miles in a buggy to the train for Duluth. Mrs. Gulbranson's hands are badly burned, for on the road she had to take her own clothing and fight flames on the children's clothes. As soon as they have enough clothing the family will return to what is left of their home at Adolph. They are at the Y. M. C. A., and Mr. Gulbranson is reported safe in the city." [200]

## Mildred Elnoea Halverson (January 23, 1903 to October 12, 1918) and Myrna Mathilda Halverson (April 8, 1901 to October 12, 1918)

I vaguely remember my mother speaking of the tragic deaths of two Hermantown sisters as I read an article from the Duluth News Tribune and looked at its grainy photograph of two teen age girls. Several people who wrote their memories mention the two sisters. Gordon Velander wrote that the house next to his family home had two teenage daughters who hid in their house and burned with it. Delaine Carlson noted that her mother, Alice Walin, had gone to school with some girls who died from going into the root cellar where they were suffocated and died.

"Two more victims of Saturday night's conflagration will be buried this afternoon at 1:30 o'clock at Hermantown Cemetery. Mildred and Myrna Halverson were burned at their home in Hermantown, left with no avenue of escape and completely surrounded by walls of impenetrable flame."[201]

Another newspaper told more of the sisters and their story. The Duluth News Tribune of October 17, 1918, had a subheading, "Halverson Funeral." "Funeral of Mildred and Myrna Halverson, sisters, of Hermantown, who were found dead in the basement of their home, will be conducted this afternoon at the Lutheran cemetery by Rev. J. J. Daniels, pastor of the Swedish Mission Church. No services other than those at the cemetery will be held.

These two girls, the daughters of a prosperous farmer, have lived at Hermantown all their lives. They are graduates of Ensign High School, and Mildred was attending Central High in Duluth up to the time of her death. They lived in a beautiful home which was completely destroyed by fire. Mildred and Myrna both have a large circle of friends and their home has often opened wide its doors for merry weekend parties, the destination of bob parties, for a hot oyster stew and

199 "Mortuary Notice: Deaths," *Duluth News Tribune,* December 29, 1918. On line at GenealogyBank.com. https://www.genealogybank.com/doc/newspapers/image.
200 Lucille M. Pearson, *History of Fredenberg; 1887 to 1981*, page 40.
201 "Hermantown Victims," *Duluth News Tribune,* October 17, 1918. Online at GenealogyBank.com. http://www.genealogybank.com/gbnk/newspapers/doc

the scene of many gay gatherings.

The girls are survived by their father and mother, Mr. and Mrs. H. Halverson, two sisters, Mrs. G. Johnson of West Duluth, and Miss Alma Halverson, a teacher in the Jackson School, two brothers, Halvor Halverson of West Duluth, and Harold Halverson, who is in the United States Navy." [202]

In a Duluth News Tribune column listing those dead by cemeteries, Mildred Halverson and her sister, Myrna, were listed as being at Filiatrault's Mortuary. Added was the following sad note: "These two sisters were found in the basement of their home."

## Aino Hatinen, Son of Ole Hatinen

Another very young child perished from the Fires. Although I at first thought this was a youngster from Thomson Township, I was informed this past summer that this was not the same toddler. Linda Soderberg Hatinen discovered that a little boy of that approximate age who died in Thomson Township was Samuel Henry Hatinen, son of Abel Hatinen and Eva Ruuskanen Hatinen. Thus, the Aino Hatinen, son of Ole Hatinen, appears to be from another family.

"Aino Hatinen, aged two and one-half years, son of Ole Hatinen of Hermantown, another fire victim, died at St. Mary's Hospital yesterday *[i.e., October 23, 1918.]* Funeral arrangements have not yet been made."[203]

## A Fire Memoir from Ruth Carlson, (1899 to 1983)
### (Mother of Jim Heffernan of the Duluth News Tribune)

The following story I initially read and clipped from the Duluth News Tribune of October 12, 1998. It is a part of the memories of Ruth (Carlson) Heffernan, the mother of retired Duluth News Tribune featured columnist and published author, Jim Heffernan. On the 80th anniversary of the 1918 Fires on October 12, 1998, he wrote a column in the Duluth News Tribune telling about his mother's memories of that fateful day, titled, "It Was a Day to Remember." Although his 19 year old mother's home was on Piedmont Avenue between Third and Fourth Streets in the West End, her recollections speak about what was happening in Hermantown during the Fires. As he writes in his book, *Cooler Near the Lake,* "This is my mother's Cloquet fire, as she told the story often, once a couple of years before she died in 1983, into a tape recorder." [204] (His mother's account of the Fires is included in a collection of his enjoyable newspaper columns, *Cooler Near the Lake,* which can be ordered at the blog he maintains: www.jimheffernan.org.)

*It was a very lovely sunshiny day. It was a Saturday and I had baked several loaves of bread. My friend and I went downtown in the afternoon to look for a birthday gift for another friend. We left about 2:30 and went to Wahl's Store, which was George A. Gray Company then. (After shopping) when we came out on Superior Street a terrific wind was blowing and it was very dark. We boarded a streetcar and coming up Piedmont Avenue we met trucks with people on them screaming. Balls of fire were rolling down the avenue, paper and other debris burning. We were very frightened and hurried to our home. (At that point) we hadn't heard what had happened.*

*The wind was so strong you could hardly breathe. I got home and my family was very excited. My mother had died in April so it was my father and five (younger) sisters wondering where to go. People were driving down Piedmont Avenue in trucks and cars, screaming. They had been picked up in Hermantown where everything was on fire.*

---

202 "Brief, Private Funerals Held for Fire Dead. Numerous Victims Given Interment in Duluth by Rushed Undertakers. Halverson Funeral," *Duluth News Tribune,* October 17, 1918. Online at GenealogyBank.com. http://www.genealogybank.com/gbnk/newspapers/doc.

203 "Two More Fire Victims Die in Duluth Hospitals," *Duluth News Tribune, October* 24, 1918. Online at GenealogyBank.com. http://www.genealogybank.com/doc/newspapers/image.

204 Jim Heffernan. "It was a Day to Remember," *Cooler Near the Lake: Fifty-Two Favorites from Thirty-four Years of Deadlines,"* (X-comm, Duluth, Minnesota. Printed in Brainerd, U.S.A., by Bang Printing), p.172.

*Soon a friend of ours called and told us to pack clothes and little food and be ready to flee down to the bay because Duluth was surrounded by fire and (he said) the bridge crossing to Superior was burning. The Woodland area was also burning. A neighbor came over crying and wringing her hands because her three children were visiting in Lakewood with their grand-mother. She didn't know if they were alive.*

*Then we heard they had ordered the people from Twelfth to Tenth Streets and the area all around there to vacate. There was so much smoke we could hardly breathe. The rooms were filled with smoke. They called my dad and asked if he would take the grocery truck from where he worked to Hermantown to pick up people. He couldn't leave us alone.*

*(Later in the evening) my younger sisters were sleeping and my dad and I were up watching. About 2 o'clock in the morning the wind died down. We were saved—how thankful we were. My friend and I walked up to Hermantown the next day. What a sight we saw---people weeping standing in front of ash piles that had been their homes…so much sickness, too…. the people were dying from the flu (The fire occurred during the great Spanish flu epidemic.) It was not a pretty sight to see beautiful trees and vegetation all black, but the people were brave and went back to their small farms and started to build again.*

*It was a day to remember.*"[205]

Ruth's future husband, also from the area, was in the Army and stationed in San Francisco. Imagine his anxiety when he read San Francisco newspaper headlines declaring that Duluth, his home town had been almost destroyed by fire. His relief must have been great upon learning from his parents and siblings that most of Duluth had been spared. [206]

## John Hendrickson

An early newspaper report presented the fight against the flames of an exhausted but victorious man.

"From the Village of Pike Lake to Hermantown, every farm building is leveled until John Hendrickson's place is reached. His farm and two others between there and the crossroads are all that remains of Hermantown. At the crossroads only a church is left standing. Cattle, horses and chickens are running loose everywhere in the district. John Hendrickson was hardly able to talk. He could not see because he had fought fire all night to save his home, and the smoke had temporarily blinded him. Fire swept along through the grass to within less than 10 feet of the house. Patches of a barn roof were burned off. Every farm around him was destroyed. Yet he had saved his few little buildings, his three horses and his chickens. He was completely exhausted." [207]

## The Bernhard and Rena Jacobson Family, Daughter Eleanor, and Son

### Helmer Jacobson (November 26, 1913 to November 3, 2006)

Written by Connie Jacobson

My father, Helmer Jacobson, was a month shy of his fifth birthday on that fateful day, and his baby sister, Eleanor, was about three months old. Dad remembers being hoisted into the horse-drawn wagon and fleeing the farm with little more than the clothes they had on their backs. Although he wanted to take the little wooden wagon his carpenter father (Bernhard Jacobson – 3-25-1889 to 2-20-1973) had recently made for him, there was no time, and they had to leave it behind, as well as almost all of their photos, and even his beloved pet dog and cat. Previously his father had chased the

205 Jim Heffernan, *Op.cit.*, pp.173-174.

206 *Ibid.*, p. 174.

207 "Dead Found Lying by Roadside. Hermantown Loss," *Duluth News Tribune,* October 13, 1918. Online at GenealogyBank.com. http://www.genealogbank.com/doc/newspapers/images.

cows, pigs, and chickens out of the barn and into the open fields, to do their best at fending for themselves, in the vain hope they would survive.

As fast as the horses would safely carry them through the choking smoke, the windblown ash, embers, and flames, they left their farm on the Rose Road, heading west to the Midway Road, and from there to the Miller Trunk, parts of which were then called the Swan Lake Road and Pike Lake Road. Many times the family members had to beat embers and small fires out on their clothes, the horses, and the wagon and its contents, on their hazardous journey to the relative safety of West End community of Duluth and the immediate shelter of family. They had no way of knowing that the central part of the city of Duluth would not burn as they fled, and if necessary they would seek the safety of the waters of Lake Superior.

The Miller Trunk was so smoky and visibility was so limited that Grandfather just held the reins in his hands and let the horses lead the way amongst the cars and other horse-drawn wagons. Baby Eleanor was weakly coughing and had a great deal of difficulty breathing, and her mother, Rena Anderson Jacobson, (1-4-1886 to 7-14-1976) was afraid her infant daughter would suffocate.

Finally, the frightened horses reached the safety of Duluth's West End and the house of Grandfather's sister. Only at that time did Grandfather relax enough to let the horses' reins out of his hands, to see them virtually disintegrate into ashes! Needless to say, the entire family had minor burns, but was very thankful to have made it alive, having seen dead and dying people and animals around them on their perilous journey.

One of the most poignant memories I have of my father was hearing him speak of coming back to their burned out farm, after the fire, and looking for his little wagon. "It was all burned and gone. Nothing was left. The few cows that hadn't been burned alive, were stumbling around, half burned, and bellowing in pain. Pa had to put them out of their misery."

Thankfully, Grandfather was able to use his carpentry skills to quickly build a so-called "Red Cross Shack" to house them through the oncoming winter. Dad's childhood was spent in poverty, as the family tried to claw back from losing everything. Although the fire had burned all structures around the entire immediate area, some salvageable but fire-killed trees were left standing. Grandfather and Dad harvested those for years afterward to use in rebuilding and other purposes. When I would go skiing back into the woods in back of our house that adjoined my Grandparent's land, I saw a six foot tall remnant of a large white pine stump at the back corner of the 10 acres my parents owned. This was during the late 1950s and early 1960s, and I can still picture it in my mind, with a tongue shaped scar left from the flames of 1918.

My grandparents themselves didn't want to talk about the fire since it traumatized them so greatly. Grandmother's family was living in the farm country around Rice Lake, Wisconsin, from whence she hailed, and a cousin told me her family had some replacement portraits made. The family was especially saddened by the loss of the large wedding portrait in the fire, from 1913. Relatives on both sides of the family gave spare pieces of furniture and Grandfather also built some.

When I was growing up in the late 1950s and 1960s, I remember conversations between my parents and their friends, most of who had grown up in Hermantown and survived the 1918 Fire. They always worried about dry weather during the late summer and early fall of the year and another potential conflagration. Even then I remember them making reference to events as occurring either before the Fire or after it. My mother (Evelyn Witte Jacobson – 3-21-1917 to 1-5-2005) remembered friends and neighbors who had burns on their legs and arms that pained and scarred them for the rest of their lives. Dad's life-long friend, Bertil Erickson, had lost a baby sister, Marie Charlotte Erickson, in the Fires.

Even now I get a shiver thinking about the Fires! And dry warm weather in the fall of the year always reminds me of that October so long ago, and I shudder.

Photo of Helmer Jacobson, sitting in rocking chair his carpenter father built, holding his pet cat, with his pet dog, in front. His mother wrote on the back of the photo, "Helmer at Time of Fire," and I presume it was taken the summer just before the 1918 Forest Fires destroyed their house.

(October 5, 2011; major revision August 20, 2013. October 5, 2011 version appeared in the Hermantown Star. Revision is unpublished.)

## Aurora Janzig
### (April 5, 1912 to October 13, 1918)

Little Aurora Janzig died the day after the Fires as a result of her burns in St. Luke's Hospital. A newspaper listing gave her name as being deceased and at Fred Olson's Mortuary. [208]Several Hermantown residents remember hearing that she was found in the basement. Her grave is located at the Hermantown Cemetery on the Morris Thomas Road. [209]

Photo of grave and marker for what is believed to be the resting place for Aurora Janzig. From FindAGrave.com — used with written permission from photographer. Added by: Cathy R. 9/19/2013. [210]

## Arthur Johnson

Arthur Johnson's remarks of the Fire were recorded in a newspaper article. His last sentence serves a reminder that World War I was still raging overseas.

*Late yesterday afternoon Arthur Johnson of Hermantown completed the task of digging the last of 600 bushels of potatoes and other vegetables, the summer crop. The crop was stored, and return for the months of hard labor was at hand. Shortly after unhitching his team, the fire appeared, and in a few minutes he was forced to harness his team and with his family fly for safety. As he left the barn yard the barn with his one cow, and summer's crop burst in flames.*

*"Hermantown Is All Gone"*

*"Hermantown is all gone," said Mr. Johnson last night. "And I feel confident that there was a heavy loss of lives, because of the rapidity with which the fire came, and the effort to save too much. It was about 6:45 that*

---

208"Known Dead-Duluth List," *Duluth News Tribune,* October 15, 1918. Online at GenealogyBank.com. http://www.genealogybank.com/gbnk/newspapers/doc

209 Cathy R., added information and photos on 9/19/2013 to "FindAGrave.com." She wrote, "Please include the following notation 'From FindAGrave.com – Used with written permission from photographer.'
This is so others know to check out FindAGrave for more information."

210 "Settlers True Blue; Want to Pay for Bonds. Burned Completely Out, Farmer Orders Lumber and Makes Plans to Rebuild," *Duluth News Tribune,* October 16, 1918. Online at GenealogyBank.com. http://www.genealogybank.com/gbnk/newspapers/doc.

*we first noticed the fire, and within 15 minutes it was closing in on the place. It is a funny sight to see great sparks falling and threatening one's entire worldly goods. It reminded me of falling stars. I harnessed and started for town with all speed. When I got to the West End [of Duluth, a/k/a Lincoln Park] the horses were 'all in,' so I asked a passing car to take the folks. I turned the horses loose, so do not know whether I will ever see them again or not. I have hunted high and low for my family but have not found them as yet. But I am sure they are safe, and I have my strength left, so it is better than a German invasion anyway."*

## Mrs. Clara A. Johnson
### (February 1876 to October 12, 1918)

While some survived the Fire by fleeing to root cellars, others met their death in them.

"Smothered to Death. Mrs. Clara Johnson, Maple Grove Road, north of Duluth Heights, was smothered to death in a root cellar at her home in which she sought refuge from the fire." [211] She is buried at Oneota Cemetery in Duluth.

## Emil Johnson

Mr. Johnson's patriotism and resiliency was noted in a Duluth News Tribune article four days after the Fires. The descriptive title was "Settlers True Blue; Want to Pay for Bonds. Burned Completely Out, Farmer Orders Lumber and Makes Plan to Rebuild." Emil Johnson was referred to as only one example of the many settlers who still insisted on paying for Liberty Bonds, despite the fact they had lost almost everything.

"Emil Johnson, a farmer on the Pike Lake Road near the Jackson School, met Maj. H. J. Mullin yesterday. He spoke of his Liberty bond pledge, newly made, he said. 'I can't make my payments right now, but I'm going to.' Major Mullin assured him that others undoubtedly would fill out the quota of those who had sustained great loss. 'No, I'm going of take care of my own obligation,' Johnson replied. 'The government needs that money. I'm going right back to farming, and I'm lucky to have my farm. Lumber is coming, and when it gets here I'll build a little shack and start going again.'"

## Johan August Johnson
### (December 23, 1860 to September 28, 1993)

A newspaper article briefly mentioned a fire loss in the Adolph area to a J.A. Johnson. "J.A. Johnson lost his farm buildings and eight head of cattle burned to death in the barn." [212]

However, in an e-mail from John and Nancy Nordin in August of 2017, I learned more about the J. A. Johnson referred to in the newspaper article. As Nancy wrote, "The J. A. Johnson referred to in the Adolph Losses article was John's great grandfather, Johan August Johnson, who was living on the farm along with his wife Lovisa (Andersdotter), October 28, 1860 to October 19, 1933), daughter Ida (Elvira Johnson) Bjorlin, August 16, 1885 to April 29, 1967, her husband Carl, and their two children - Florence (Louise) Bjorlin (July 14, 1910 to January 13, 1989, and Wendell (January 1, 1916 to July 13, 1937). I do have photos of the farm before the fire and then one of the 'new' house, built in 1920. This still stands. The bluestone basement is original, pre-1918. There's an old root cellar in the front yard, but completely covered by soil & turf...have never seen it and wonder what it holds?"

---

211 "Smothered to Death," *Duluth News Tribune,* October 13, 1918. Online at GenealogyBank.com. http://www.genealogybank.com/doc/newspapers/image
212"Charred Embers Only Left in Adolph Munger District," *Duluth News Tribune,* October 15, 1918. Online at GenealogyBank.com. http://www.genealogy-bank.com/doc/newspapers/image.

Farmhouse that burned down in the 1918 Forest Fires of the Johann and Lovissa Johnson family, in Adolph.
*The photo is from the personal collection of great grandson, John Nordin.*

Farmhouse built in 1920, on foundation of house that burned down in 1918 Forest Fires, of Johann and Lovissa Johnson family, in Adolph. Note the lack of trees or foundation shrubbery, especially compared to their pre-Fires house.
*The photo is from the personal collection of great-grandson, John Nordin.*

## Carl Walfred Bjorlin

### A Son-in-Law of Johan August Johnson, (February 9, 1885 to May 20, 1964)

In August of 2017 a son and daughter-in-law of Florence (Bjorlin) Nordin (7-14-1910 to 1-13-1989) were kind enough to e-mail information her son, Michael Nordin, had collected from his paternal grandmother by conducting an oral interview with her about the 1918 Fires. Michael Nordin, a descendant of Adolph Bjorlin, was interviewed by C. M. Falk of the *Hermantown Star* in July of 1993. He spoke with pride of the same land being in his family for over 100 years, and was photographed in front of the house built after the 1918 Fires. One of his grandmother's vivid memories he enjoyed hearing about and picturing in his mind was the blacksmith shop on the land. Before that fateful day in October of 1918 the farm ". . . looked like a little city," Mike wistfully remarked. The Fire changed all of that, however, and in a hurry! His grandmother told him the winds were so strong that entire trees and large limbs were coming into the house. Furthermore, she remembered the wind blowing so violently that whole trees, on fire, were landing on the roof. His grandmother escaped to the Proctor Roundhouse in a car that had over twenty people piled in and on it, with some people on top, and others on the hood. [213]

In 1918 Florence Louise Bjorlin was 8 years old, living with her parents Ida and Carl Bjorlin, and brother Wendell Bjorlin in Proctorknott. On October 12, 1918, however, Ida, Florence, and Wendell were visiting Ida's parents, Johan August Johnson and his wife, Lovisa on their farm in Adolph.

*Eight year old Florence, her mother Ida Elvira (Johnson) Bjorlin [8-16-1885 to 4-29-1967] and a two year old brother, Wendell, [1-1-1916 to 7-18-1937] were visiting the Johan and Lovisa Johnson farm in Adolph when they received word (as well as looking at the sky) that the firestorm was soon to be upon them. The father and husband, Carl Bjorlin, was a fireman working aboard the Duluth Missabe and Northern (DM&N) train and apparently was part of the manpower trying to rescue people along the route. Mother Ida's brother, Arvid Johnson, [3-5-1896 to 4-7-1989] lived close by and was responsible for coming to their rescue, piling people into and onto his car, as he took them to the Proctor Roundhouse. The farm burned to the ground along with the horses, and whatever other livestock they had. When the family was able to return to their property, Florence said she remembered the SMELL . . . "It was burnt meat and baked potatoes!" The potato crop had been brought into the basement for the winter and as the bluestone basement was all that was left, the potatoes had survived. When we built a home on the adjoining property in the late 1970s we still saw the huge burnt stumps bearing witness to that terrible fire, and that was 60 years later!"*

As of 2017, John and Nancy Nordin have two items in their possession that survived the Fires: a shears; and a Blanke's Coffee tin box in which the family's essential documents were kept. John said his great-grandfather used the tin as a safe for important papers, and he tucked the box under his arm as he fled the fire. The blackened shears, which still work, were found in the ashes of the house.

213 C.M. Falk, "Same Land's been Home to Family for Over 100 Years," *Hermantown Star*, July 15, 1993, pp. 3-4.

The photograph was taken by John Nordin in August of 2017, of his great-grandfather's tin coffee box in which he stored documents. It was photographed on a wooden windowsill of the family's barn, built after the 1918 Fires. His great-grand father grabbed the box of precious papers as he fled the farm, threatened by flames.

Photograph of blackened shears taken by John Nordin, on weathered wood of the barn rebuilt after the 1918 Fire. The shears were found in the ashes of the home. Although the heavy, blacksmith's hand crafted shears had been burned black, they cleaned up well and still worked perfectly in 2017.

## Mary (Erickson) Johnson and Gustave Johnson

**(Mary-1868 to April 3, 1920)**

The Gust Johnson family lived at Five Corners, but, according to a Duluth News Tribune article, ". . . was burned out in the big forest fire. Since then they have been living in Duluth." [214]

At the time of her death she was 52 years old and living with her husband at 2318 West Eighth Street in Duluth. Her funeral occurred at her Duluth home and the Swedish Mission Church at 21st Avenue West and Second Street. She is buried at Union Cemetery, on the Hermantown Road. She was survived by her children: Mamie Johnson, Esther Johnson, Edith Johnson, and Clarence Johnson, as well as her mother, Mrs. Harry Erickson.

214 "Mrs. Mary Johnson, Pioneer Resident of Duluth, Dead," *Duluth News Tribune,* April 4, 1920. Online at GenealogyBank.com. http://genealogybank.com/gbnk./newspapers/doc

## The Anton Klosowsky Family, by Granddaughter Alice Martini

### (Anton Vincent Klosowsky January 18, 1845 to October 12, 1918; Amelia Beyer Klosowsky, April 10, 1852 to November 3, 1918)

The tragic tale of the Klosowsky family was documented by one of their granddaughters, Alice Martini, and presented by Melvin Martini at a meeting of the St. Louis County Historical Society at Denfeld High School on January 14, 1931. The brief section referring to the Fires is preceded by a detailed and wistfully wonderful description of Hermantown as it was before the 1918 Fires.

*The forest fire of 1918 took with its toll my grandfather and my grandmother. My grandfather was killed in a wreck the night of the fire, and my grandmother died three weeks later from wounds and burns received during the fire....Together they played, together they worked, and together they died under the hand of the same fate in 1918.* [215]

August Klosowsky, an older son who lived in Two Harbors, Minnesota, apparently spoke to the newspaper staff of that town, *The Journal News*, shortly after his father's death. He left for Hermantown two days after the Fire, to tend to his seriously burned and hospitalized mother and little brother, as well as his deceased father. August said that the team of horses were apparently spooked by a flame of fire and refused to go, sending the wagon over a 50 foot embankment. His father was killed instantly, but the rest of the family was picked up somewhat later by a passing car and brought to Duluth for medical care.[216]

A great-granddaughter of Anton and Emilie Klosowsky also described her great-grandparent's tragic death in the 1918 Fires.

*Anton and Emilie Klosowsky – their farm was in the . . . Hermantown area. They had 3 girls and 9 sons. One was Henry Klosowsky – my grandfather. One of the younger sons, Ben, was at home at the time. He got Anton and Emilie in the horse (one or two horses?) drawn wagon and tried to outrun the Fire. When the Fire closed in around the wagon, the horses ran wild and the wagon crashed – crushing Anton. Ben carried his mother – running and managed to get help. Emilie died of smoke inhalation. Ben was burned severely and was deeply scarred for the rest of his life. Ben, like several of his brothers, worked for the railroad. He was given a desk job and then pension for the rest of his life. With the total loss of both farmhouses, etc., [Patricia refers to the Fichtner and Klosowsky homes] all family records were destroyed. Anton and Emilie came from Prussia as young people and met in church.* [217]

"Bud" Wagner also told of the Klosowsky tragedy in his unpublished autobiography.

*The Klosowskys got in a buggy and headed for Duluth but when they got as far as Wheeland's [Wieland's] Dump the horse either stumbled or fell as there were other pile ups and the horse and buggy fell over on Mr. Klosowsky and he was killed. Mrs. Klosowsky was badly burned and died . . . later. The son who had come up that day from Duluth to check on his folks was badly burned and lived, but spent almost a year in the hospital.*[218]

215 Alice Martini, "Klosowsky: the Family Genealogy. The Story of My Grandparents Life in Minnesota." Unpublished paper, a copy of which is retained at the Hermantown History Center.

216 Carol Illikainen, *Firebeast: the Fires of 1918,* published by Moose Lake Area Historical Society, 1994, and republished with corrections and additions in 2016, pp. 46-47.

217 Patricia Gregory Op.cit.

218 Wilmar "Bud" Wagner, "Wagner's Autobiography: the 1918 Fire," unpublished autobiography, a copy of which is retained at the Hermantown History Center.

Photograph of Klosowsky Marker in Hermantown Cemetery on FindAGrave.com

Laura (Manske) Sundquist wrote about her relatives, the Klosowsky family. An excerpt is taken from her unpublished manuscript.

*<u>Ernest's Farewell – 1918:</u> War clouds hung heavily all over America. In Hermantown, many young men had been drafted, so when Ben Klosowsky's name came up, because he was married and had a child (Marion), arrangements were made with the Draft Board that Ernest Klosowsky go in his brother's place. Ben moved back home to help his parents maintain the farm.*

*On that day in August of 1918, when most of Ernest's family gathered to wish him well and to say good-bye, there was not a thought that the First World War would end soon. There were many mixed emotions and much sadness. However, with America sending many men and much armament, in less than three months the day of Armistice came (on November 11) and in due time, Ernest returned home.*

*The forest fire of October 12, 1918, had destroyed the Klosowsky home—his father killed instantly—his mother badly burned and living only three weeks. Ben also suffered greatly in the Fire as he tried to drive his parents and himself to Duluth for safety from the flames.*

*Luckily, Hulda and their baby daughter, Marion, had stayed at Frank and Freda's for a visit over the weekend, and so avoided being in that awful night!* [219]

The death certificate lists Anton Klosowsky of the Morris Thomas Road as being 75 years, 8 months, and 24 days old at the time of his passing, with the cause of death being described as "Crushed under his horse when attempting to escape forest fire."

His wife, Amelia Klosowsky, died less than a month later. An announcement from the Duluth News Tribune of November 8, 1918, entitled, "Klosowsky Funeral," reports the following: "The funeral of Mrs. Amelia Klosowsky, 66, who died at her home near Hermantown last Sunday, will be held at 2 p.m. this afternoon, from Olson & Hoppanyan undertaking rooms. Burial will be in Hermantown cemetery. Mrs. Klosowsky was badly burned in the forest fires of Oct. 12. Her father lost his life in the flames and her son Benton, age 23, was severely burned. Twelve children, nine boys and three girls survive." The children were Anna, Emelia, Odelia, John, August, Anton, Michael, Conrad, Henry, Frank, Benjamin, and Ernest. [220]

---

219 Laura (Manske) Sundquist, unpublished manuscript, retained by daughter, Winnie (Sundquist) Gustafson.
220"Klosowsky Funeral," *Duluth News Tribune,* November 8, 1918. Online at GenealogyBank.com. http://www.genealogybank.com/gbnk/newspapers/doc.

## Mary LaCourse

**(c. 1858 to October 12, 1918)**

Born Marie Beaurivage in Quebec, Canada, she married Eustache Paquette, with whom she had seven children. Thus, in the 1900 Federal Census she was listed as Marie Paquette. However, in 1902 she became Mrs. Firman LaCourse, and they lived at R.F.D. 2, Box 64 in 1917 with two of her pre-teen sons from her first husband. Apparently she was the only one of the family who perished in the Fires.

## Nikolai Larsen

**(November 25, 1857 to October 12, 1918)**

His wife, Nilsine, as well as his three sons and two daughters, survived the Fires. However, he did not. He was reported to have died in a field on the Maple Grove Road, and is buried at Oneota Cemetery in Duluth.[221]

## The Edward Lawyer Family

**Edward (c. 1858 to October 12, 1918), Ida Acker Lawyer (August of 1868 to October 12, 1918, and Son Edward, 1908 to October 12, 1918)**

Although no written notes or memories have been located about the Lawyer Family, the tragic deaths of the entire family can only be imagined. Edward Lawyer and his wife, Ida, were active and fairly prominent members of the Hermantown community, with their productive farm on the Hermantown Road. Presumably, their only child, Edward, would have followed in his father's footsteps, had he survived. Several newspapers of the decade speak of Edward Lawyer and his successes.

Ed Lawyer moved from city of Duluth to the countryside in Hermantown, and was so successful that he had an article written about his farming successes in the local newspaper.

"Ed Lawyer, a son of German immigrants, had a 40 acre farm on the Hermantown Road, from which every few days he brought a load of produce into Duluth. He grew strawberries, which he sold in Duluth, as well as radishes. Additionally, he was a dairy farmer, milking Guernsey cattle. He was reported to be doing so well that he had to increase the size of his barn and install a hay carrier to handle his hay crop. Reportedly, he started farming in Hermantown in 1901 amongst the stumps. Even though he had worked since 1888 for the grain elevators in Duluth, he gained knowledge of farming on his own and worked out problems for himself."[222]

In 1913 Edward Lawyer is again mentioned in a newspaper column in connection with farming. The Farmer's Produce Club was an organization of settlers in the vicinity of the Washington School in the Township of Herman. Officers were as follows: Edward S. Lawyer, President; Otto Witte, Vice President; Gust Lueck, Secretary; and F. W. Ruhnke, Treasurer. (Other members listed were John Potzin, Ben Klosowsky, J. H. Grady, Charles Wittich, Henry Wagner, and Leo Witte.) [223] Later that same year, he, as President of the Hermantown Farm Producer's Club, issued a statement that the farmers were very satisfied with the support given them from the people of West Duluth who bought their produce at the West Duluth market. [224]

---

221 Collene "Family Finder," added to FindAGrave.Com, on July 2, 2014.

222 "Truck Farms Near Duluth. Ed Lawyer, a Grain Elevator Worker, Goes into Gardening and is Successful," *Duluth News Tribune,* July 1, 1911. Online at GeneaologyBank.com. http:www/genealogybank.com/doc/newspapers/image.

223"Farmers Club is Organized. Settlers in Town of Herman Form Organization to Promote their Welfare," *Duluth News Tribune,* May 23, 1913. Online at GenealogyBank.com. http://www.genealogybank.com/doc/newspapers/image.

224 "Farmers Pleased with Success of Market," *Duluth News Tribune,* November 17, 1913. Online at GenealogyBank.com. http://www.genealogybank.com/

Things were apparently going well for the Lawyer family and those farming the land in the Township of Herman. However, a catastrophic event intervened that would change the area and its residents forever. The next time Edward Lawyer was mentioned in the press would be the last time. Tragically, the 60 year old Mr. Lawyer, his 51 year old wife Ida, and his 6 year old son, Edward, perished in the 1918 Forest Fires.[225] The entire family is buried at Forest Hills Cemetery in Duluth.

## Victor Leslie
### (1865 to September 16, 1946)

"Victor Leslie, a widower who lived on a farm south of the Miller Trunk Line and west of the Jackson School, saw the fire about 5:00 P.M. He had planned to go into Duluth on Saturday to sell a load of wood, but because of the fire danger he did not want to leave his children alone. Leslie stayed on the farm hauling stones to clear land and doing other chores. By late afternoon he went to telephone around to find out if the fire had blown up. He also went south about a half mile on the Ugstad Road, where he met Mrs. Charlie Anderson and two children. She was crying because the fire was approaching her house, and he went to see what he could save. When the fire came right up to the house, he had to leave. As he put it, the "fire came just as fast as we could run," and the "sparks and the flames was all over us." He had to hurry home to save his three children. Leslie had been a sailor about forty years earlier but he had never seen such a fierce wind. The flames were right over his buildings, coming out of the northwest when he left. Leslie made his way north with family, his horses, and his cows to the green area along the Miller Trunk Line below Pike Lake. By 5:30 or 5:40 they were safe, but all of his buildings and those of his neighbors were destroyed. At night, after the main fire had passed, Leslie went into Duluth." [226]

## Oscar Carl Lindahl
### (January 21, 1888 to November 10, 1918)

Only a brief announcement of Mr. Lindahl's death mentioned his fate. The title, "Oscar Lindahl, Hermantown Refugee, Victim of Influenza," summarized the last month of his life. Apparently he was burned out of his home, and died at St. Luke's Hospital following an attack of influenza on November 10, 1918. "He was formerly a resident of Hermantown," the announcement concluded. His draft papers for World War I in 1917 list him as being a single farmer, who supported his widowed father, Ole Lindahl. The address was given as RFD #1, Box 107, as it also was in the 1918 City of Duluth Directory. His remains are buried at Scandia Cemetery.

## Doris Constance Lofald
### (March 3, 1911 to March 12, 1990)

In 1931, Doris Lofald articulately preserved her vivid memories of the 1918 Fires in writing for posterity. At the time of the Fires her family consisted of her parents, Michael Lofald and mother Kristine Hagestad Lofald; siblings Agnes, Millard, Victor, Myrtle, Irwin, Grace, and Waldemar.

*Thirteen years ago, on a Saturday afternoon, it was nearly dark at 2:30 p.m. But it was not the ordinary darkness of after*

---

doc/newspapers/image.

225 "Known Dead—Duluth List," *Duluth News Tribune,* October 15, 1918. Online at GenealogyBank.com. http://www/genealogybank.com/doc/newspapers/image.

226 Francis M. Carroll and Franklin R. Raiter, "The Fires Above Duluth," *The Fires of Autumn: The Cloquet Moose Lake Disaster of 1918*, page 68, 1990, Minnesota Historical Society Press, St. Paul, MN.

*sundown. There was a terrible blackness at the horizon and every object was weird looking. Smoke was in the air, stronger even than it had been during all the week. Up in the sky, the sun could not even be seen through all the smoke. The western sky, however, was illuminated by a horrid, gruesome, sparkling glow reaching from the horizon up to the high heavens. The fire was then within 10 miles of us—and no way of escape was in sight. The winds brought us the smell of burned buildings, burned soil, burned animals, and even bodies of humans that had been burned and who could not escape this terrible sweeping fire, which devastated every object within its path. The wind was blowing at considerable velocity, which made destruction even more imminent.*

*We became especially alarmed because at this time no way of escape was open to us. Father and one of the boys we knew were on their way home from town, seven miles away, and nearly a whole day's trip. They weren't due to arrive until about 4 o'clock. All we could do was wait. Of course, they had seen the approaching fire and hurried the horses as much as possible. Finally they did come, and I can remember as though it were yesterday, that they drove the wagon up to the house instead of to its usual place and we immediately began to load into it whatever we thought most valuable and necessary to save. We later found, however, that we took many things of little importance, and in our frenzy overlooked many things we should have taken. I remember, too, just how the wagon was parked—with the front wheels slightly turned, as if ready to go with only a word. From this time on, until we were started on the road, I can't remember much very distinctly. There was so much fire all about us, and smoke, and excitement. It was a new experience for all of us, and one I hope never to see enacted again, for anyone. As we drove out of the yard, we all looked back on the house and our big spruce trees standing nearby, rather knowing we would never see the same again. I know the older folks must have had a terrible sinking feeling as we all drove away and left our home at the mercy of those sparks and flying burning sections of buildings. I wasn't old enough to share the sense of desolation they must have had.*

*I can remember faintly our trip into town, with the big white horses, Queen and Maude, steeping quickly, almost at a trot, pulling the heavy load with all of us in it, and loaded heavily with household articles. The horses' manes were flowing, and their ears held up alertly. The smoke and fire was all about us, and it was by this time (4:30) quite dark, so dark we could hardly tell each other apart in the wagon box where we all sat. When we left home we had quite a bit of food—I remember especially a number of loaves of bread Mother had just baked, and we took it from the table where it was cooling. We also had a jar of butter along, which we put in one of the water pails. Looking at it later, it was all like hot soup, from the heat of the fire about us. As sparks went by, some of them lit onto the horses' manes and in their hair and we had to stop to put water on or otherwise put out the spark, and one time a burning piece of timber came flying and landed among our blankets and quilts and we simply threw overboard the burning mass of flames. As we looked back before making a turn in the road, we could look back and see our neighbors' buildings aflame.*

*Down on the hill, just entering town, we had a narrow escape as in the darkness the horses, wagon, and all of us, nearly went over the high bank, but due to the quickness of the horses and the driver, we got back on the road safely, feeling thankful for our escape. Surely God watched over us all that night.*

*We finally reached our aunt's house. I remember how surprised they were to see us, and I remember that we were all so sick and tired and smoky and dirty—we must have been almost unrecognizable after our several hour battle against sparks and smoke, trying to protect ourselves as well as our belongings, and throwing out the burning pieces and parts of houses that landed in our box. Even whole parts of roofs and long boards were sailing by, carried by that strong western wind. By the time we got to town, everything was in bad shape; what wasn't burned and thrown out was covered with black coals and ashes.*

*I never shall forget that night. I, for one, went to bed hungry. I remember too all the beds were taken and Wally and I slept in back of the heating stove in the dining room, with only half-burned quilts over us. I also remember I was cold during the night and early morning as the fire had gone down. I didn't recall whether we went to bed dirty or if we had been washed, but I know we were very tired—yet we talked some about what had just happened before going to sleep. This was all so sudden and strange to both of us. I'm sure that as we said our prayers that night we all thanked God for His care in a more meaningful way than ever before.*

*The next morning Father and the boys went back home—and yet not really "home" because our home was gone. Only a smoking heap of ashes and debris in our basement remained of what yesterday was a 2-1/2 story dwelling. I can scarcely imagine the feelings they must have had to see nothing there by the foundation on which the house rested, some smoldering embers, and a heap of ashes.*

*The rest of us did not go out there for quite a while. The men had to sleep in the hayshed, which for some reason, was not burned. Then in due time the Red Cross helped to furnish "shacks," which were just that. Because there were so many of us in the family, we got two—one we called simply "the shack" and the other the "paper shack"—the latter name because of the paper board walls, I suppose. As time went on, they were made more livable, but they were not much to start with. We as children did not mind or complain, but it must have been a letdown for the grownups.*

*Then immediately after Father and the boys got home, they were all sick with the flu—the war-time influenza—with no one to take care of them. We, in town, were also sick, and Wally and I both had a touch of Diphtheria, I think it was. I remember being in town on November 11, 1918, the day of all the hooting and howling and parades, and celebrating, and we looked out of the window.*

*The problem of clothes to wear now confronted us. We got garments from different people, and the Red Cross, also some girls in New London. Most of them had to be made over, and even at that we felt foolish in most of them.*

*One day some people came by with their electric car. This was something we hadn't seen before. I must have been sick in bed at the time, or else there wasn't room for me, but at any rate I didn't get a ride in it. Nobody knows how bad I felt that I couldn't have gone along. If they only knew. I felt so bad that to this day I haven't gotten over it.*

*I remember one day when I was lying in bed, someone came to see me and brought me one of those flat tin boxes of Perfectos, I think they were called. I thought they were the most delicious of anything I had ever tasted. I remember even the different flavors. I kept the tin box for years.*

*I hastily remember Mrs. Dahl sitting by the bed, having come to see me. It might have been she who brought the delicacy to me.*

*Then the day we had word that could come "home" again. It must have been sheer bravery on Mother's part to go out there and start all over again from almost nothing. Patiently, she made the best of everything, doing without things she had been used to, and putting up with all sorts of inconveniences, with no place to put anything away. It must have been terrible not to have any towels or linens or dishes or decent clothing. But Mother always saw to it that we had enough clothes to wear—for warmth even though not variety. I know we always had clean clothes.*

*I remember a lot of things that happened, and the conditions under which we lived during those six years or so that we lived in those "shacks." We put up with a lot, and did without a lot, always patiently waiting for the time when we could put a house on that foundation again. It was a long wait, but I think even to this day I can appreciate it all the more because of not having had a nice house for so many years.*

*That Forest Fire of October 12, 1918, marks a dividing line in our memories—reckoning something was either "before the fire" or "after the fire"—unless it happens to be "at the time of the fire."*

*One thing for which we all are everlastingly grateful to our God above is the fact that we all escaped without a burn or any loss of life, and some families were not so fortunate. We lost all of our material possessions except the very clothes we wore and the few articles we took with us, but we kept the things that count most. Our family remained intact, which means more than anything else. Truly earthly things pass away, but God's Word will not pass away."*[227]

227 Doris Constance Lofald, "October 12, 1918, as I Remember It," 1931, unpublished manuscript retained at the Hermantown History Center.

## Simon Luczak Family
**(October, 1855 to December 12, 1957)**

Simon Luczak, his wife, Mary, and three children were staying at the pump house at Five Corners, a newspaper report stated. [228] Since their farm was on the Maple Grove Road, they apparently weren't too far from their homestead.

Although Josephine Luczak was not here for the Fires she recalled stories told to her by her husband, Peter, and her father-in-law, Simon. During the Fire, Simon Luczak had his family leave their farm to head towards Duluth before him. He soon hitched up the horses and began the perilous journey to Duluth. However, he only made it to a nearby river because the wooden bridge had burned. Simon and the horses spent two days in the river, wondering what had happened to the all their farm buildings. Upon return his heart sunk, because the entire farm had burned down, with stone foundations for the barn and other buildings being the only unburned elements. When the rest of the family returned they found Simon crying for what they had lost. The Luczak family was helped by the Red Cross after the fire and lived in a nearby unoccupied substation for three years. The family soon gathered and rebuilt a new farm on the property, where it remains to this day. [229]

## Erick Lundberg Family
**(April 20, 1875 to June 18, 1946)**

Adolph settlers Erick Lundberg, wife Mary, and children Harold, Edwin, Andrew, Hjalmer, Melvin, Herman, and Mary K. suffered heavy material losses as a result of the fire.

"Erick Lundberg, storekeeper at the village *[of Adolph]* was probably the heaviest loser. The fire not only destroyed his store and stock, but also his farm house and all machinery." [230]

## John Joseph "Jack"McGovern and Family
**(March 5, 1871 to November 20, 1938)**

It's difficult to imagine a family spending an entire night in four feet of cold water in the bottom of a well, but that was what the McGovern family did. The family consisted of John McGovern, his wife Emma, children Mary, Benjamin, John, Michael, Mabel, Margaret, Mildred, Eugene, and Phillip.

"Mr. and Mrs. Jack McGovern and family of nine children of Hermantown escaped the fames by spending the entire Saturday night in a well on the farm, there being four feet of water in the well." [231]

## Milton Magnuson
**(Adolph Milton Magnuson: February 19, 1902 to March 1, 1985)**

Milton Magnuson briefly recalled that dreadful night of flames six decades later.

---

228 "Additional Refugees Not Previously Reported," *Duluth News Tribune,* October 15, 1918. Online at GenealogyBankl.com. http://www.genealogybank.com/gbnk/newspapers/doc.

229Janelle Erickson, "The Catastrophic Fire of 1918 Leaves Lasting Impression on Many Area Lives," *Hermantown Star,* August 31, 2001.

230 "Additional Refugees Not Previously Reported," *Duluth News Tribune,* October 15, 1918. Online at GenealogyBank.com. http://www.genealogybank.com/doc/newspapers/images.

231 "Proctor Cares for Suffers from Country. Searchers Find Dead and Pitiful Cases of Distress—Courage Shown by Refugees," Duluth *News Tribune,* October 16, 1918. Online at GenealogyBank.com. http://www.genealogybank.com/doc/newspapers/images.

*"We just barely escaped with our lives," recalled Milton Magnuson. "There was no other thought." The Magnusons had a brand new home in 1918, in fact. "The painter's tools were still there, I remember. I was out in the field not aware of the danger until the high wind began building and then the fire hit. We hitched horses and got to Proctor where we stayed overnight. The next morning, there was not a speck of wood left on any building, just piles of ashes."*[232]

## Ludwig Johann Manske and Huldah (Kohlts) Manske

### (Ludwig-March 24, 1855 to June 24, 1939; Huldah-September 6, 1865 to October 14, 1935)

Until the time of the Fires, they had lived on a farm in Hermantown. However, after the Fires they moved to the West End of Duluth around 27th Avenue West. Since they were both in their 60s, perhaps they didn't want to start over again with farming, and instead moved to the city.[233]

## Otto Paulus Eberhard Nelson and Theodora (Benedicta) Nelson

### (Otto-March 5, 1877 to January 23, 1948; Theodora-April 8, 1878 to January 3, 1962)

The interesting and detailed memories of the Nelson family were preserved in a book available at the Hermantown History Center, entitled, *The Book of Esther: For Such a Time as This. Based on the Memories and Writings of Esther Nelson Hallock.* A sizeable section of the book refers to the 1918 Forest Fires. Esther Florence Nelson (Mrs. Leonard Hallock) was born June 10, 1916, and remained very alert and vigorous until her passing on February 10, 2015.

***1918***

*On the morning of Saturday, October 12, 1918, my mother, Theodora Nelson, had set some bread to rise and decided to go to town for some supplies. While it was a beautiful autumn day it was very dry and windy. With a family of 9 children and a husband, a trip into Duluth, Minnesota was always an exciting and rare event. She had my brothers, Erling and Art, hitch up their horse, King, for the trip. She left behind my sister Essie, her oldest, to stay home with the younger children. My father Otto and my two older brothers, Otto Jr., and Bernie, had left at 5 a.m. to work on a farm further north.*

*They saw some small fires along the road but didn't pay much attention to them because brush fires were a very common occurrence. They had no sooner gotten to town when there was a call to the grocery store that there was a fire at Five Corners which was just 10 miles from our home. So she hurried and got 100 pounds of flour and a box of soap. She said she had wanted to get some fruit but decided she had better rush home. She called my sister Essie and told her to pump some water into some tubs.*

*On the way home, she stopped at her father-in-law's house in the West End of Duluth. It was around noon when my mother called the store at Five Corners and was told things were looking bad. She started home at once.*

*At first when they started home it was clear and sunny so they thought, "Why hurry?" But as they got closer to their home, it looked very different and they saw fire in the trees. She got all her children into the wagon and decided to drive to her brother Emil's place to see if it was safer. The only things they took with them were a watch and some war bonds. She had planned to go back because they had left behind her dog and pups in the house. However, when she got to her brother's house and they looked back toward their home, several fires seemed to explode round about, like bombs of fire. Her brother told her it wasn't safe and that they needed to go someplace else; so they got in the wagon with the horse and went to Pike Lake Road*

232 Anne Stultz Bailey, "Wind and Fire, an October Holocaust!" *Duluth Budgeteer Special Edition*, "Wind and Fire, an October Holocaust!" July 18, 1979.
233 William Kohlts e-mail to author dated October 23, 2013.

*heading for Duluth and Lake Superior. Since Duluth is situated right on the shore of Lake Superior many people were headed for the lake. During the fire that day the wind shifted and Duluth was spared.*

*While on the highway, a car came along. It was someone she knew but he could only make room for my Mother and the four smallest children, Art, Einar, Pete, and me. The cars on the road were very loaded driving into the city. They were bringing all the people they could possibly carry. Cars were coming out from the city to pick up people as well. My mother said there were times when there were fires coming from three different directions, and she was pretty nervous about being in the car because the smoke was so thick you couldn't see. She was afraid they would go off the road, and she was very worried about my sister and the boys. Essie, Ted, and Erling kept driving with the horse but they had to gallop to keep ahead of the fire. My brother Erling said that although King was tired from the 18 mile round-trip to town and back, he seemed to find new life. He said that they got to a point that they could no longer see the road and they all lay down in the back of the wagon. My sister said that she let go of the reins because the horse could sense where the road was better than she could. King guided them to safety.*

*I remember that time very well although I was so young. My mother got to the city just fine and to my Grandfather's house and then of course, she had a really tense time. I think I can remember standing with my mother, just standing in her skirts, the wind blowing very hard, just standing there waiting for my sister and the other kids. They finally came. It was nine o'clock at night when they got to the city. My sister was running in front of the horse and wagon. We really had a very happy reunion. We took King, the hero horse, to a livery stable, and asked the man in charge if he had room for one more. He said he had about 50 horses but he could make room for one more. We later heard many got caught in the smoke and went off the road.*

*It was a terrible night for the whole family because nobody knew where my father and brothers were. At 5:00 a.m my mother went to the police station to see if they had heard any news. They told her that many people burned to death on the road. She stayed awake all night. The next day I think she went to the Red Cross and someone said they had seen this tall, dark, handsome man (which he was) with two teenage boys. When she went back to my grandfather's house they were there. We really had a happy reunion when we realized that all eleven of us were still alive. My father told us they had been trapped behind the fire and blockaded. When they were finally able to get to the house there was nothing left but a charred field and two haystacks. The haystacks were the only things that didn't burn. Apparently the fire was carried by the wind and just flew over them. My mother always had lots of pets but the dogs were gone, all the chickens and cattle. It was a pretty desolate scene for my father and brothers to find. They had no idea we had escaped. He told her how terrible the fire was up the road. He said he had been very afraid. He was so happy to find his family all safe.*

*There was, however, a lot of tragedy. Two of our neighbor's boys perished. They found the 14 year old, or what was left of him, after searching for a couple days. The other boy was 21 but he was so badly burned he only lived for sixteen days. There was a mother and a baby who were desperately trying to get a ride in a car. The car was so loaded they couldn't take one more person. They were afraid the car would stall if they put too much weight on it. So this mother threw her baby into the car, and of course the people couldn't refuse the baby. Because she was relieved of the weight of the baby she was able to run fast enough to keep ahead of the fire. She was later reunited with her child. The cars that were driving to Duluth and towards Lake Superior had their lights on because the smoke was so thick you couldn't see. They were all following the taillights of the car ahead. There was a curve in the road and when they got to the curve, one of the cars went off the road and the other cars all followed. Many people were killed in the pile-up or burned and unable to escape. {Note: This was on the Miller-Trunk Highway.}*

*In a book called Burning an Empire, author Stewart Hall Holbrook says that during the fire the wind that night rose to 76 miles an hour. Not since records were kept had 76 mile an hour winds hit northeastern Minnesota before. He said that the Duluth News-Tribune stated that 453 people died during the fire and another 85 succumbed to burns, making the total death toll 538.*

*My mother's brother, Emil, had been riding on the running board of a car when he fell off and had to crawl in the middle of the road for a while. He suffered burns and couldn't see for a few days. Before he left his house, he grabbed an extra pair of pants. Those pants saved him because he threw them over his head when the flames passed over.*

*Art's wife, Violet Carlson Nelson, said that her family got into a well to escape the fire. While their family lived, another family had done the same thing only to perish when the well cover caught fire and came down on them. Ted and Erling's wives were sisters, Inez and Ethel Lindberg, and they lived in a town where so many people perished that their father had to help plow trenches to bury them.*

*My parents had built a wonderful home on a piece of land with beautiful trees. Now it was all gone. After the fire people were very kind to us. We stayed at my grandfather's house for a few weeks. We had some war bonds and made a deposit on an old, cold house and lived there over the winter. We had a family picture taken not long after the fire because we were all so happy to be alive and together. All the clothes we were wearing in that picture were donated to us by the Red Cross.*

*The owner of the Big Duluth Men's clothing store gave my dad and seven brothers each a pair of shoes. Our family never forgot that act of kindness. From that time on, until the owner died many years later, my dad and brothers never shopped at any other store for their suits and shoes.*

*(Winter after the fire)*

*That Christmas Eve there was nothing in the house to eat. So my mother sent my sister Essie out to get some potatoes and fish. While she was gone, the Red Cross came with a box of oranges and apples and with a present for each of the children. They also gave us a wood burning stove. We had a Christmas we would long remember. Other people brought clothes and vegetables during that difficult winter and I don't know how we got through it. The family was so grateful for the kindness of people who came forward to help.*

*We had to start all over again that spring. My father cut the black burnt trees and then he and Ted hauled them to the mill and got lumber to build a one room cabin where he stayed alone while working on the property. Later, mother went to the Red Cross and got more lumber so he could build a house for the family. Eventually we did build on the new land, and with left-over lumber, he built a small barn where we could put a cow.*

*The next project was building a three-room house. There was a kitchen with a large table, a wood cook stove, shelves for groceries, barrels of flour and sugar. In the root cellar, which was a dirt excavation with a step-ladder to climb down, we kept potatoes, carrots, rutabagas, beets, etc., all of our harvest plus crocks of homemade jams. After the fire, wild strawberries and blueberries flourished in the burned out areas and we used to take our lunch pails and pick berries all day.*

*My mother, when she later wrote of this experience, had this to say. "Before the fire we had a pretty nice home with lots of stuff in the cellar - all of it was destroyed. Our cows and horse were taken care of that winter at the community stables. Erling stayed and worked there while Art stayed with my brother Emil. We were very comfortable. It was homey and we even had a pond in back of the house. The boys had a lot of fun bathing in it and we skated on it in the winter. I really don't know how we got through it all. But believe me when I say, you have to have faith in the Lord, and when you do, you find out you can go on with very little."*[234]

## Tekla Linea Nelson

**(September 27, 1914 to March 27, 2014)**

Tekla Nelson was one of the survivors who rode out the Fires in a potato field, covered with wet gunny sacks. She was living with her parents (Ellen Gulbranson Nelson and John Nelson) and maternal grandparents (Olaf and Emma Gulbranson) in the Midway Township area, very near the boundary of Adolph and Midway Township.

234Sandra Reinke and Colleen MacDonald, *The Book of Esther: For Such a Time as This. Based On the Writings of Esther Nelson Hallock*, 2006, pp. 51-57.

The photo shows the ruins of what used to be their house, with burned debris in the foreground.
Notice the horse drawn wagon on the driveway in back of what had been the house.

*The photos are courtesy of Hermantown Historical Society and member Mary (Olson) Milbrath.*

## Arthur and Selma Olson

Although the farm buildings of Arthur Emanuel Olson (February 1, 1894) and Selma (Lindquist) Olson (1892) were devoured by the Fires, many of the trees were left standing. Daughter Mary (Olson) Milbrath noted the house was just at the end of the Lindahl Road. Depicted is the driveway leading up a small rise to the spot where their house had been.

## Peter and Clara Olson Family

Even the lives of those born shortly after the Fires were affected by it, as was noted in the obituary of a Hermantown resident.

"Blanche was born only a few weeks after her parents and brother narrowly escaped the Great Cloquet Fire. The house that they had newly built, intending to move into with the new baby, burned to the ground." [235]

(Blanche Olson married Robert Benson, and became Blanche Benson.)

## C. Parson, Mail Carrier

A local mailman was also directly affected.

"Here are a dozen men in the service of the Duluth post office who have either lost members of their family or their houses, but not one has missed a day of work since the fire. All are diligent in serving these unfortunates in the prompt dispatch of mail, was the statement of Postmaster W.E. McEwen yesterday. Those in the postal service who suffered losses are . . . C. Parson, the Hermantown rural carrier. . ."[236]

## Mrs. Fred Peterson (Anna Peterson)

One of the fatalities in Adolph was briefly noted.

". . . Mrs. Fred Peterson, aged about 60 years, was overcome by smoke and her life was snuffed out by the flames before assistance arrived. Mrs. Peterson lived with her family on the E. Bjorlin farm." [237]

## William Schuman and Henry Schuman

The William Schuman family consisted of wife Anna, and sons Julius and Henry. However, only William and Henry were listed as being at St. Luke's Hospital in Duluth. The address of the family's farmstead was listed in the 1910 census as R.F.D. (rural free delivery) No. 2, which appears to be a Hermantown address. William was approximately 59 years old, Anna was about 42 years of age, Julius was about 18, and Henry was 14 years old.

---

235 Obituary of Blanche (Olson) Benson, *Duluth News Tribune*, September 15, 2013.

236 "Dozen Mail Men Suffer Loss of Homes, Stay on Duty, "*Duluth News Tribune*, October 17, 1918. Online at GenealogyBank.Com. http://www.genealogybank.com/doc/newspapers/image.

237 "Known Dead-Duluth List, "*Duluth News Tribune*, October 15, 1918. Online at GenealogyBank.com. http://www.genealogybank.com/doc/newspapers/image.

## Mrs. Mary Soderholm

**(1862 - 1946)**

Lengthy newspaper articles from those early days contained information about people in the area of the Fires. One of those families was mentioned several times.

Mary K. Magnuson had married John A. Soderholm in 1900, but was widowed in 1914, left with five young children. For almost two weeks in the local newspaper in November of 1914, a want ad was printed to sell her late husband's sawmill. "FOR SALE –At a big bargain, complete, small sawmill with engine & boiler, located at Adolf, [sic.] Minn. Mrs. J. Soderholm. Adolf, Minn." [238]

The first brief status report is from October 14th, and simply lists Mrs. Mary Soderholm and five children, of Adolph, as being "Others Accounted For." [239]

Another brief status report hints at the family's experiences. The next day it was reported that Mrs. Mary Soderholm had "Gone to Adolph. Will be back." [240]A separate column from that same day further stated that, "Three children, Mrs. Mary Sederholm [*viz.]* (mother and father) Adolph, do not know where they are going."[241]

Since my mother remembered Mary Soderholm as the kindly woman who invited her and her brother in to her house to warm up on their walk to the Lincoln School about a decade after the Fires, she and her children apparently went back to Adolph.

## Charles and Louise Stahbrodt

**(Charles, 1857 to 2-18-1926)**

**(Louise, October, 1863, to April 14, 1919)**

Charles Stahbrodt was such a successful gardener that he merited both a newspaper article as well as a photograph of his greenhouses. The article praised him as being one of the most successful market gardeners in the district. It continued to say that he received half of his income from his greenhouses, whose area totaled 4,500 square feet. The photo pictured his glass houses in which he grew fresh vegetables for the local market from November until May, as well as starting tomatoes and other plants for summer gardens in his fields.[242]

With his large greenhouses and attractive farmhouse on the vicinity of the Haines Road, he and his family had a lot to lose when the Fires of October 12th struck the area. All of his family then living with him at that time, consisting of him, his wife Louise, daughter Edna, and son Clarence, survived the Fires.

However, his wife, Louise Stahbrodt, died six months after the Fires. The funeral notice in the newspaper stated that her health was affected by the Fire. A little less than eight years later Charles himself passed away.

'Mrs. Louise Stahbrodt Dies; Health Affected During Fire.

---

238 "For Sale," *Duluth News Tribune*, November 5, 1914, through November 17, 1914. Online at GenealogyBank.com. http://www.genealogybank.com/doc/newspapers/image.

239 "Refugees Registered in Duluth. Read Them and Help Reunite Fires' Stricken Families," *Duluth News Tribune,* October 14, 1918. Online at GenealogyBank.com. http://www.genealogybank.com/gbnk/newspapers/doc.

240 "Additional Refugees Not Previously Reported," *Duluth News Tribune*, October 15, 1918. Online at GenealogyBank.com. http://www.genealogybank.com.doc/newspapers/image.

241 "Additional Refugees Not Previously Reported," *Duluth News Tribune,* October 15, 1918. Online at GenealogyBank.com. http://www.genealogybank/com/gbnk/newspapers/doc.

242"Greenhouses are Important in Gardening," *Duluth News Tribune,* October 30, 1909. Online at GenealogyBank.com. http://www.genealogybank.com/gbnk/newspapers/doc.

Mrs. Louise Stahbrodt, age 65, wife of Charles Stahbrodt, died last night at the home of her daughter, Mrs. N. Wiedmark, on R. F. D. 2, Duluth. Deceased had been ailing since the forest fires. She is survived by a husband, Charles, the daughter and one son, Carl. Funeral services will be held tomorrow at 2:30 p.m. at the home of her daughter. Interment will be at Union Cemetery."[243]

## The Stebner Family

(Frederick: 1835 to 1925; Raymond P.: June 4, 1908 to November 20, 2002; Herman: 1878 to May 5, 1936; and Fred: February 18, 1901 to October 17, 1985)

The Stebner family of Hermantown had their experiences in the Fires noted in several newspaper articles a few decades ago. Among Stebner family members whose memories were quoted were Frederick Stebner, Herman Stebner, Fred Stebner, and Raymond P. Stebner. Ethel (Stebner) Witte, would be born a little less than three months after the Fires.

*The tragic 1918 fire totally destroyed many Hermantown farms and Herman Stebner lost his house and buildings, but Grandfather Frederick was able to save his. With characteristic determination, the Stebners began the long, slow process of rebuilding. Their truck garden brought income from the Duluth market for a time and they were able to, with the help of others members of the family, acquire a few cows and a horse. They also continued the dairy business for a time, which became known as the Northfield Dairy, making deliveries downtown as well as throughout Hermantown.*

*"It was the most beautiful morning you ever saw" is how Ray Stebner remembers the morning of October 12, 1918. He was 11 years old. "The sky was crystal clear. Dad and I planned to take the horse and buggy 14 miles to Fish Lake to go fishing. It was a big work horse, I remember, and when we smelled smoke we stopped and tied the horse, deciding not to proceed to the lake but to look around for the fire. We could see it coming through the woods, coming up fast. We let the horse loose and ran for a nearby root house. There were little kids in there that we helped save from suffocation. By the way, they remember that to this day."*

*There was no warning system for the settlers and when the fire hit, it was with a roaring onslaught. Fred Stebner described "balls of fire rolling in the air, catching at the treetops. That's what destroyed my father's house."*

*Fred, who was 17, had been delegated with other young men to fight the fire and they were loaded on a wagon and left off at Five Corners. "The fire was so bad by then that I knew all I could do was try to work my way back," Fred said. "The fire was ahead of me and it was terribly hot because the log fences on each side of the narrow road were burning. I got as far as Grandpa Stebner's place, then walked a little farther back and saw that all the buildings were on fire at our place. I went back to Grandpa who asked me, 'How's yours?" and I said, "Gone." "You can help me then," he said. By sheer force of will and luck, Frederick Stebner, then 83 years old, and his grandson were able to save the house. "We stayed up all night," Fred said. "I'll never forget grandpa sitting there in a chair with a pail of water and whenever sparks landed, he'd throw water onto the logs with a dipper. The next morning he said, "I'm tired today, but last night I could throw a pail of water over the house!"*

*"There were 84 roasted chickens strewn around our barnyard," said Fred Stebner. They also lost all their hogs. Their cattle who had waded into a creek apparently suffocated from the smoke. "One cow was still breathing but when I touched it the hide came off." The Stebners stayed the night of the fire in a tent on the Westberg place, and "You could hear the wolves howling all night. They were hungry. The next morning we didn't need a stove to make coffee, just put the pot on a smoldering pine stump."* [244]

243 "Mrs. Louise Stahbrodt Dies; Health Affected During Fire," *Duluth News Tribune*, April 15, 1919. Online at GenealogyBank.com. http://www.genealogybank.com/gbnk/newspapers/doc.
244 Anne Stultz Bailey, Duluth *Budgeteer Special Edition*, "Wind and Fire, an October Holocaust!" *Duluth Budgeteer Special Edition*, July 18, 1979.

## Ole T. Stene, wife Carolina Stene, and son, John Stene

**(Ole, 1860-1932; John born 1897)**

The Two Harbors newspaper, *The Journal News,* reported that they were living on a farm eight miles outside of Duluth on the Hermantown Road. They hitched up their horse to a wagon and reached Duluth safely, but lost everything on the farm. In the aftermath of the Fires they stayed with their daughter, Mrs. Leonard Stube. [245] Their address was a R.F.D. box address corresponding to the Hermantown area in 1917, although previously they lived in Duluth. Apparently they lived at their farm only a year or two.

## Laura (Manske) Sundquist

**(July 12, 1905 to October 23, 1991)**

The following excerpt is taken from an unpublished paper written, in beautiful and perfect penmanship, by a young Winnifred Sundquist for her ninth grade English class. Her mother, Laura Sundquist, had lived through the Fires and reminisced often about her past in Hermantown. Winnie was interested in history even as a child, and for an assignment wrote about the history of Hermantown as related by her mother. What follows tells about Laura (Manske) Sundquist's memories of the 1918 Fires, as written by Winnie (Sundquist) Gustafson.

*The community which was growing and prospering was given a great set back in 1918. The summer had been a dry one. No rain had fallen for months. Smoke could be seen rising from swamp fires as if to warn people of the coming disaster. On the afternoon of October twelfth a strange red glow appeared in the sky. The air became stifling with smoke. A strong wind began to blow and soon flames could be seen. The fire, which started in Cloquet, swept rapidly over the dry land. People became panicky, some even thinking that the end of the world had come. Some started by horse for town. Others went into underground root houses, hoping to escape the flames. Many ran to plowed fields where they dug in and kept wet blankets over them. By four o'clock the sky was as black as midnight, and a seventy-five mile an hour gale was blowing.*

*The next morning looked upon a sad sight. Though a few farms remained untouched by the fire, most of the countryside was burned to the ground. A large number of lives had been lost and many were seriously injured. All those that survived were taken to town with nothing but the few possessions that they had been able to save.*

*The Red Cross came to the rescue of those left devastated by the fire. They built small temporary houses for those deprived of homes. They also gave food, clothing, and other necessities to the people. The Cloquet railroad company, which was held responsible for the conflagration, paid insurance to those injured.*

*Several years went by before the vegetation began to grow back again. Slowly the birds and animals returned, and life began again as it had been before.* [246]

## Evelyn Mable Ugstad (Mrs. William Gansauge)

**(February 22, 1909 to September 20, 1984)**

Evelyn Ugstad wrote about the history of her family and her life in the young Township of Herman in April of 1979, which she titled, "My Recollections". A copy of the unpublished story is retained at the Hermantown Historical Society's History Center. The following memoir relates her family's harrowing ordeal and heart-breaking experiences in the 1918

245 Carol Illikainen, *Firebeast: The Fires of 1918*, published by Moose Lake Area Historical Society, 1994, and republished with corrections and additions in 2016, page 107.
246 Winnie Sundquist, "Hermantown," an unpublished paper handwritten by Winnie for her ninth grade English class in the mid-1940s," pages 3 and 3A.

Forest Fires. Her parent's 30 acre farm was located just south of the Seville Road, presumably very near the border of Hermantown and Canosia Township.

*We had very little rain during the summer of 1918 and everything was very dry that fall. Our farm was bordered on all sides by timber. About 150 feet west of our house there was a large grove of birch trees. I will never forget the Saturday of October 12, 1918. There were a lot of fires in the neighborhood, and the wind was from the northwest, strong and warm. The sky was covered with smoke and the sun looked red all the time. My father went out and fought fires as there were many nearby. My Aunt, Livey Erickson, phoned my mother about noon and said there was a big fire coming our way from the west. She was so frightened. So my mother wanted to pack our new clothes that we had bought for the winter, and get ready to move to Duluth for protection, as many of our neighbors had called and suggested. But my father said, "Don't worry! We will be okay. Go ahead and clean house as usual. We will be all right."*

*He then harnessed our horse Teddy and hauled two big barrels up to the house and filled them with water to protect the house if necessary. There came many men to our place to get water to drink as they were fighting the fires. There seemed to be fires all around us. About 3:00 P.M. or so it got as dark as night, as the smoke was so thick. Our cows all came to the barn door and my mother went out to let them in the barn. My brother Reinhardt who was eight years old, said, "I don't think you should put them in the barn. If it gets real bad, it would be best to leave them outside." So my mother didn't put them in. The cows and calves, about twelve in all, bellowed at the door. My father had put our horse Teddy in the barn when he left to fight the fire.*

*There came a large dark cloud from the Northwest. It roared and flashed lightening like a thunderstorm. My mother was so happy for rain to come, she told us children to get down on our knees and she prayed and thanked her Father in Heaven for the good shower of rain. We then went into the house. My mother and brother Reinhardt and I helped to get our good clothes together and put them on the bed ready for a fast departure. I remember my mother had baked 15 loaves of bread and the floors were all scrubbed clean. I packed the bread in some school bags that we were given at the fair a short time before. My mother pulled down the shades of the windows so we wouldn't be so frightened looking at the fires around us. She really thought it would rain soon.*

*We heard a terrible roar. My mother went to the kitchen door which was on the east side of the house. When she came back in, her face was snow white and she said, "Evelyn, Rein, help me! The whole roof is on fire! Help get the kids, we have to get out!" She then fainted and fell to the floor. I took a dipper of water and threw it into her face, and then gave her a drink as soon as she came to. We gathered the children together. But my brother Art who was two and a half years old was missing. I had always been afraid to go into the living room when it was dark, so my brother Reinhardt went to look there. I went into the bedroom to look, but we could not find him. Finally Reinhardt went into the living room again and found him asleep on the sofa. He awoke him and we all went to the kitchen door. In the meantime I kept throwing water in my mother's face to keep her from fainting. My mother took us all together at the door and she told us to yell as loud as we could. So we screamed and screamed. The fire was all around. The roar we had heard and the clouds we thought were rain, was a cloud of fire. It sure did roar when it hit that grove of birch trees west of the house.*

*We were screaming all we could and the next thing I knew, my father came to us and said, "Hold on to each other and go to the wagon shed. It won't burn so fast because it is a new building. Go now! Go!" So we went to the wagon shed which stood a short distance southeast of the house. I carried the baby Linnard who was ten months old, and we all held onto my mother's skirts. There were Linnard, ten months, Art, two years, Martin, four years, Olga, six years, Reinhardt, eight years, and myself, nine years of age.*

*The wind was so strong that it lifted us up from the ground at times. The heat and smoke were terrible. Fire was all around us. We children were all barefooted. When we opened the little door at the Northwest corner of the wagon shed, the wind blew in with us as we entered. We had a small room on the end of the wagon shed for the chickens. They were all sitting on their roost. It was day but it was so dark. The wind blew in so hard that it blew many of the chickens right out the south window. We could not shut the door. On the east end of the building there were two large doors hanging on rollers on an overhead track. Of course the wind blew them straight up in the air. They stayed up there and flapped like huge wings. My mother in desperation gathered us all under these doors and hoped they would jump off of the track and fall down and kill us all. She thought that it would be better to be killed by the doors than to be burned to death. They did not fall.*

*Leaving us in the wagon shed, my father ran into the house, which was in flames, to save what he could. Of course he couldn't find the clothes as my mother had put everything on the bed. He next tried to get the bureau drawer where all the valuable papers, jewelry, etc., were kept, and of course the drawer was gone. My mother had placed it on the kitchen table, ready for fast departure. He then thought to save the cream separator. We had not had it long and it was new. He put the tank and fittings on the floor and ripped the bolted separator from the floor. He took it outside but when he tried to return the fire was so hot he had to retreat from the heat and flames. As the smoke and heat forced him back he grabbed an old wood skirt of my mother's from Norway, and an old coat.*

*When he returned to us, being fearful that the doors would fall down and kill us, he took us a little distance south of the wagon shed. He had us lie down on the ground and he lay down on top of us and protected us with his body. My father had on a wide brimmed wool felt hat, and he put his head with this hat on, toward the worst force of the wind, smoke, and fire. My mother said, "What of Teddy?" My father said, "I have been to the barn and Teddy is down. He went down with a groan as I opened the door. Oh! This is terrible. Stay down. Cover the children." My mother put her head up and found a burning piece of bark on my father's back. It had burned through his shirt and suspenders. She swept it off with her hand, and he said, "Never mind me. Just help cover the children." My mother said, "If you burn, we will all burn. Kids, dig into the ground. Throw all the dirt you can." And we all dug with our hands and threw soil as fast as we could. That is what saved our lives. There was a large hole in the ground where we laid. After the fire many neighbors and relatives came and looked where we had fought and dug for our lives. It was hard, rocky, sod bound ground. Our nails were worn way down and we sure had sore hands. Of course our bare feet and our hands were covered with burns. Our faces were so black that we could hardly recognize each other.*

*While we were on the ground a chicken came and crept under my mother's skirt. My mother finally let her stay after pushing her away many times. She said, "Better she suffocate than burn." We saw all our buildings burn. We heard the guns and ammunition go off with bangs. My father had a lot of dynamite in the wagon shed and that went off with a great many explosions as well. I cried and said, "Oh, now the Germans are coming too. What shall we do?" When the wagon shed and some lumber stacked nearby burned the heat became so intense that we had to move. My father had us crawl on our hands and knees, with our faces close to the ground so we could breathe, to a rock pile a short distance southwest. I carried the chicken with me. The cows ran back and forth near us, as fast as they could go. They bellowed loudly as they ran. I remember seeing our heifer, Nellie, run around the fire where our house had been, with her tail straight up in the air. My father kept us crawling steadily, a little at a time towards the west. He was trying to get us moved toward the places where fire had already burned. We moved to the south side of a big rock pile to shield us from the wind which had become so cold that we just shook and shivered so hard that we could not even talk. I remember my mother nursing the baby, Linnard, to try to warm him and stop his shivering. The only covering we had was that old skirt and suit coat that my father had grabbed in those last moments as he was forced to abandon the house.*

*The cows and calves came over to us. They mooed and tried to lick us all over. My mother and father cried and my father said, "Stakkars mine barn." Meaning, My poor children. I can remember that so clearly, even today many years later.*

*My father wanted to leave us and find help. I remember my mother and us kids were so afraid to let him go. But, he said that he had to go and see if there was anyone who could help us, and that he thought that he had heard somebody call from where our house was. He left and when he returned he brought the pail and dipper that had been hanging on the pump. He brought us water to drink, and used his handkerchief to wash the black soot and grime from our faces. He said that everything was gone. That many chickens were laying all over dead, and that he had to kill others that had their feet burned off but still lived. Many others were running around with singed feathers. My father slowly gave us precious amounts of water to drink. We were so very thirsty and our throats were very sore from smoke inhalation. My father held one of the cows while my mother milked her to further relieve our thirst and ease our sore throats.*

*My father left his very frightened family once again, walking to the Saint Louis County Work Farm, which was about one and half miles southeast of us, in an attempt to get help for his family. The cows lay down around us, and their body heat helped a little to keep us from freezing. Mid-October in northern Minnesota is not a comfortable time to be out in the elements, when barefoot and poorly clothed. It certainly was cold.*

*My father soon returned and told us the buildings at the Work Farm were partially burned, but the office buildings and several others were saved. We were welcome to go there for help. He also brought us a loaf of rye bread and a woolen blanket. That bread and the milk from our cow sure tasted good. Several people came by. They were lost and didn't know where they were. They were surprised to see us alive because they had heard us screaming and thought that we were all dead and burned by the Fire.*

*We then walked to the Work Farm. My father carried the two youngest and rest of us walked. It was tough walking. The ground was very hot and our feet were so sore. Our eyes were so sore and swollen that we could hardly see. What we did see through our swollen eyes was not a very pretty sight. All of our buildings were burned and quite a few of our neighbor's buildings were also lost. My cousin's farm, Ragnvald Ugstad, was just south of our farm and it too like ours was all burned. His horse, pigs, and cattle were lying dead in his fields, with their abdomens burst wide open. It was horrible.*

*We stayed a few days at the Work Farm, and then my cousin Gunhilde Mork Randall came from Duluth and took the four oldest children with her to town to stay with her. We were with her for about one month until she came down with influenza. Then we were forced to split up to stay with friends and her sister Martha Mork Randall. The two boys, Reinhardt, and Martin, were sent home to stay with my parents at the Fire Sufferers Relief Farm. My father was appointed as manager to take care of the fire victims' cattle that had survived the fire. Just before Christmas we were all reunited together again. Within a year my father started to build on his farm again.* [247]

## Gordon Stanley Velander and his Family
### (December 22, 1907 to November 1, 1999)

The following information comes from the files of the Hermantown Historical Society. It was written by Gordon Velander, a former Hermantown resident, in 1992. The Velander farm was located on the Hermantown Road, across from Bethany Cemetery. Gordon was 10 years old at the time of the Fires.

*"My brothers and I flew kites that day until the wind got so strong we had to quit. My father came home about four o'clock. He was selling Liberty Bonds. He said he was going to go up toward Munger to see where the fire was. He came back later and said we didn't have to worry. He didn't see any fire.*

*We had supper and were in the barn at about 5:30 p.m. They were milking the cows. I looked out the door and all at once the sky was on fire. They let the cows and horses out of the barn and I ran out on the Hermantown Road.*

*A wagon came along and I jumped on. It went about a half block and went into the ditch. I ran down the road again. I passed my older brother who was carrying my three-year-old brother. Another wagon came along and jumped on. It was the Nelson brothers. They had a wood rack on the wagon. We went about a half-mile to a swamp. The fire flames were blowing across the road. The wagon tipped over into a creek.*

*The Nelson brothers lifted the wagon up and I crawled out. The barbed fence tore my shirt and I ran down the road. I*

247 Evelyn Mabel Ugstad, "My Recollections," written in April of 1979, an unpublished manuscript, a copy of which is retained at the Hermantown Historical Society's History Center.

*passed the Carlson house (it was the Carlson Greenhouse).*

*Another wagon came along. I jumped on. When they pulled me over the top of the wagon, one of the stakes broke my belt.*

*Then a car came along and I jumped off the wagon onto the car fender. Then I heard my mother say, "It's Gordon. Now we have them all." In the car was my dad, mother, uncle, grandfather, grandmother, three brothers, and my sister. The car was a Model T-Ford.*

*Going down Piedmont Avenue, my brothers, uncle and I hung onto the back of the car scraping our feet to slow it down. When we got to Eighth Street on 24th Avenue West, my dad pulled over and fixed the brakes.*

*My aunt and uncle lived in the east end on 14th Avenue East and Fourth Street, so that is where we went.*

*We didn't do much sleeping the first night, but the second night would wake up when a streetcar went by and the reflection the lights made on the ceiling made us think the house was on fire.*

*We moved into my uncle's house that they had just moved out of.*

*The Red Cross built a cow barn on our farm to house the cattle of the people who had barns that burned down within a mile of our farm. About 25 people died that night in the fire, one of our neighbors had three family members die in the root cellar. Another family tried to hide in their well but couldn't find the ladder so they stayed on a plowed field. Their house didn't burn. The house next to us had two teen-age daughters who hid in their house and burned with it.*

*This is something I will never forget."*[248]

## Wilmer (Bud) Arthur Wagner

**(June 4, 1919 to January 16, 2014)**

The following is taken from an unpublished manuscript by Wilmer (Bud) Wagner, "Wagner's Autobiography: The 1918 Fire," also on file at the Hermantown History Center. Parts of it appeared in a *Hermantown Star* column in October of 2012.

*As Bud Wagner, who was born the year following the Fire aptly observed, "The 1918 Fire was one of the biggest interruptions of my folk's life." In October, 1918, a dry year, fires were common. There were no restrictions on burning. This day and days before the whole area to the south was smoldering when the wind started and the flames started too. Everywhere in the woods were tall evergreens and they said the balls of fire would be blown by the wind to another group of trees. Open fields weren't common then but tall evergreens were. Ma took some of the valuables from the house and Ray, who was six months old, and went outside in a sort of protected spot and spent the whole night that way. Pa kept on putting small fires out around the house mostly and tried to save other buildings too but failed at that as everything but the house burned.*

*Animals mostly saved themselves, all other homes were gone. The Klosowskys got in a buggy and headed for Duluth but when they got as far as Wheeland's [Wieland's] Dump the horse either stumbled or fell as there were other pile ups and the horse and buggy fell over on Mr. Klosowsky and he was killed. Mrs. Klosowsky was badly burned and died several weeks later. The son who had come up that day from Duluth to check on his folks was badly burned and lived, but spent almost a year in the hospital.*

*Pa and Ma said it was the worst night they could ever have lived through. The next morning the fire had gone through and they said their house was the only one that they could see still standing and you could see a long way because all the trees were gone too. Then Ma said all the neighbors came to their house to see if there was anything to eat as theirs was all gone. She said she couldn't even start a fire as the pile of kitchen stove wood had burned too. There wasn't even an axe to be found that still had a handle left in it so it could be used.*

---

248 "Velander's Memories of the Fire of 1918," *Hermantown Star,* August 31, 2001.

*Everything was chaos, and no one knew what to do. Everybody's cattle and horses were mixed with everyone elses. All the summer's work was gone, hay barns were all gone, winter was coming, and now this had to happen. Ma said that morning Frank Wagner from Proctor had walked out and taken an axe along to cut the downed trees away from the road. Proctor missed the fire almost completely. So, Frank found some wood pieces for Ma, chopped them up a bit so that Ma could at least cook coffee for the bunch of people.*

*Pa had a big pile of wood cut to stove length by the big rock that was burned and the hay barn. The barn had a driveway through the middle to unload from each side, but that was gone as well.*

*It's hard to imagine what it was like, and I wonder many times why I didn't ask more questions about the whole thing while I had the chance to.*

*There was some order to it all, though. The next morning the sheriff was in the area telling people where to go for food and what to do in general. The Red Cross was soon there as well and soon had material coming in for our barns and the Red Cross shacks for people to live in. Many people went to Proctor and Duluth to live with relatives and friends for a while until shelter was available.*

*Much of the North Country from Hinckley and up was wiped out. Cloquet was practically gone as far as Pike Lake.*

*A lot of the cows were rounded up and taken to the County Tool House for the winter. There weren't that many cows in the area but it did save those that the owners had no place for. My folks had three of them so they went and got one back so Ma had milk for her baby. Pa cut some swamp hay that wasn't cut during the summer and picked up some other hay in corners that had been left. I don't think the cow gave much milk that winter or got very fat, but it was one unusual thing that happened and I'm sure there many more. Then there was wood to cut again for winter's fuel. All the horses were rounded up and taken to livery stables in Duluth for the winter. My folks had three horses and by spring one had a foal which they sold for $125.00.*

*People had to go to Duluth to make application for food, supplies, lumber, and any supplies the Red Cross had to offer. It must have been quite a job for everyone involved as they had no transportation and no one had anything at all, but somehow they made out and the survivors at least got through. My folks said people were inexperienced insurance adjusters as well. He also said that he had put down that he lost some new net wire in the fire and the adjuster said, "Anybody knows that wire can't burn." My dad took some in his hand and it crumbled quite easily. Many tried to get more than their share. My grandparents got a Red Cross Shack, and there were quite a few of those around. They must have done a pretty good job of it all because by the time I was ten years old or so the only evidence of the fire was brush growing in Hermantown instead of tall trees like other places. I remember, though, that there were many references to the fire. One of them I can remember is the Peter Fishan family just across the road from us was completely burned out so they sold the land and moved to Duluth. The cement floors of some of the buildings remained for years and I would go there and play with all the nails that were left from the fire.*

*My dad bought thirty acres of this land and by the time he was through farming he had it all cleared out. A lot of the rocks had been dug and blasted out; small ones were picked and ditches dug for drainage. Also the concrete floors were removed to balance the rusty nails, many of which were square. A lot of hay and potatoes were grown on that land. One of the Fishan daughters used to come in the summer to buy pickling cucumbers from my folks. Both Roger and his boy Steve have built homes on twenty acres of this land now.*

*The 1918 fire was an unforgettable tragedy for my folks and anyone else who went through it. People would talk about it in later years. The green forests were gone and popple brush and other brush soon grew up. The timber was dead and much of it was lying down. Much fire wood was cut from it. Many families had lost family members as well as their homes.*[249]

249 Wilmer (Bud) Wagner, "Wagner's Autobiography: The 1918 Fire," an unpublished autobiography, a copy of which is retained at the Hermantown History Center.

## ALICE WALIN

### 1907 - 1994

### My Mother's Story of the 1918 Fire

Written by Delaine (Johnson) Carlson

Hermantown Historical Society member Delaine Carlson was able to recall her grandparent's experiences during the 1918 Fires. Her grandfather's entire farm burned. Even his insurance policy and inventory was somewhat scorched by the flames. Her father and his brother, Arthur Johnson, were in the U.S. Army, fighting in France during World War I. Another brother, David Johnson, was in the Navy and died on January 24, 1919, from the Spanish Influenza at the Great Lakes Naval Base. She continued to report that many of the able bodied men were serving in World War I and not home to help with rescue or salvaging efforts. All too often the women and children were left to their own devices to save themselves from the Fires. In the case of Delaine's grandparents, a sixteen year old, Carl Johnson, was at home, because he was too young to serve in the military. Please see the Addendum D to see a part of the involved and detailed Claim form her grandfather had to complete.

As Delaine Carlson wrote in an e-mail, "*A windy day always upset my mother and words about the 1918 fire would always be recalled as a remembrance of that horrible, windy, and smoky day in October of 1918.*

*Alice Walin, at the time of the fire, was eleven and a half years old and living on a farm in the Twig area, up Hwy #53, about 10 miles past Pike lake. They lived at the end of the Carlson Road that runs parallel to #7, where her school was located. (Her school in this present day is the New Life Church.)*

*Her father, Johan Walin, was ill with pneumonia and had been staying with grandma's sister, Hulda Leander, in the West End of Duluth. He had died the week (ten days) before the fire, on October 2, 1918.*

*Grandma was home with Alice and her sister Esther, who was almost 8 years old, and her brother Art who was 19 years old. They all noticed the sky turning color and the wind picking up. You didn't have to wonder what was coming because the smell of smoke was in the air.*

*Reports about the fire seldom relay the fact that the fire spread up through the Cotton and Meadowlands area because the same train that started the fires in the tinder dry woods and bogs along the track kept on going north to the Range Cities.*

*Grandma's fire didn't come from Cloquet, it came from the northwest.*

*On their farm they had cows and chickens. With the help of Hulda's boys they had put all their hay in the barn's hayloft for winter. While making preparations to leave the farm they figured the barn and house and other buildings would burn. However, they thought that if they put their furniture and dresser drawers out in the middle of the field, loaded with all of their clothing, maybe they could save the furniture as well as their clothes. They covered them as well, with a tarp.*

*As fires are not predictable... so was this one! The barn burned ...and the hay flew through the air and set fire to the pile they had made in the middle of the field but the house didn't burn.*

*Art had a car that they escaped in to a gravel pit somewhere near them. The smoke was so thick they couldn't see the road so Art lay on the fender and guided them by dragging his hand in the gravel road and avoiding the ditch. I don't know if it was Grandma or other neighbors driving the car.*

*There was a lake called Mud Lake just across the road from them, but there was no mention about going there to escape the fire. I know we were never allowed to go swimming there because it had blood suckers.*

*My mother had gone to school with some girls who died from going into the root cellar where the air was sucked out by the wind and they suffocated. Fortunately for my mother, her family also had one of those root cellars on the farm that they didn't use that day.* [250]

---

250 Delaine (Johnson) Carlson in an e-mail to author, "My Mother's Story of the 1918 Fire."

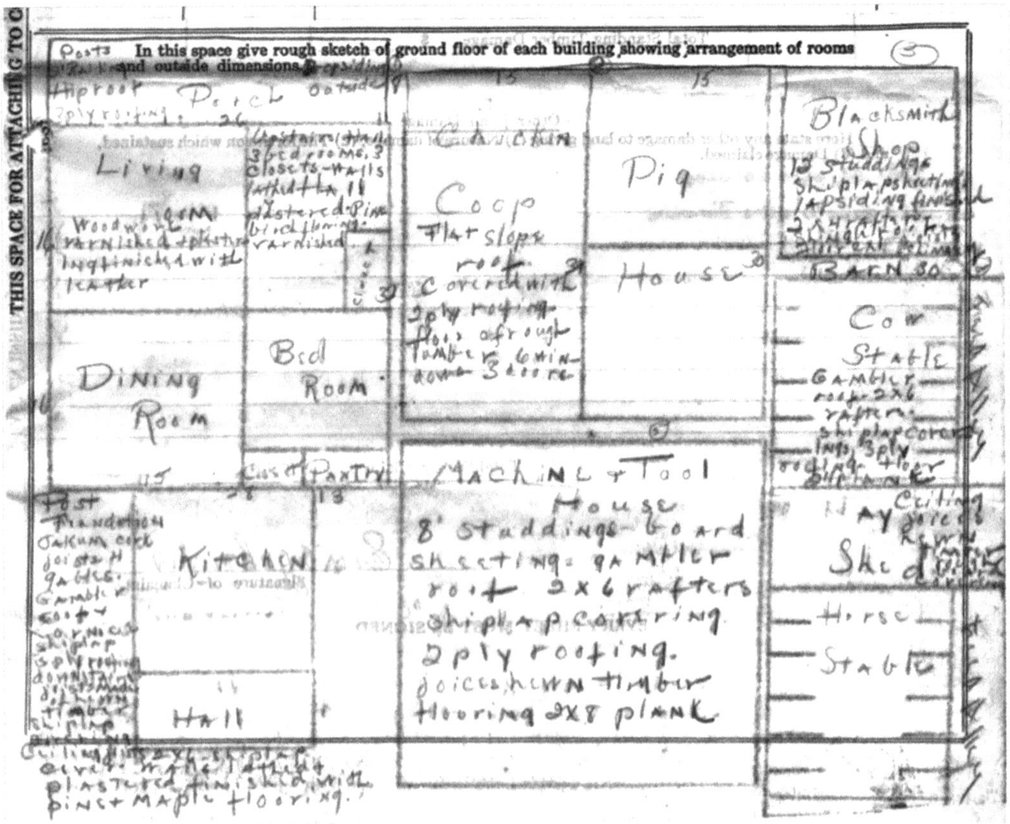


Detail taken from Verified Insurance Claim Against USA Railroad Administration for Property Damage from Fires of October 12 1918, of Emil Johnson, Delaine Carlson's grandfather, depicting the lay-out of the farm and its buildings. It lists the buildings destroyed. (The form is provided by Delaine Carlson.)

## Fred Ward

Fred Ward was the superintendent of the Work Farm. The St. Louis County Work Farm was located where the Federal Minimum Security Prison is today, site of the former Air Force Base. Being located so close to Hermantown proper and having a few of its residents employed there, it was considered to be a part of the Hermantown community.

Early on he was listed as missing, but a newspaper article four days after the Fires reported that he was very much alive and well.

"Fred Ward, superintendent of the work farm, bought a suit of clothes 'all by himself' yesterday. This means that his host of friends may now dismiss their fears that he might not recover from the effects of the fire. When a party of rescuers found the superintendent he was battling the flames at the farm, and during the many hours he had been thus engaged he had become burned on the hands, arms and face. The fire had come close to his eyes time and again, and when he was brought to Duluth there were fears that they might be found to be permanently injured. Superintendent Ward was taken to the home of Judge H. A. Dancer. Members of his family were invited to remain with friends in the West End. They had been sent away long before the fires became so serious. The work farm head may be a guest of Judge and Mrs. Dancer a day or two longer; then he expects to look things over at the farm. The old camp was destroyed, but the bulk of the new buildings were not burned. When Mr. Ward was in the downtown district yesterday he caused considerable surprise because of the general impression that his injuries were of a grave character. It was explained that his clothes had been practically burned off and that this condition required him to substitute the borrowed garments for those that would fit better. A. D. Wilson of St. Paul, a relative of Superintendent Ward, telegraphed an inquiry as to his welfare and until the superintendent's actual appearance it was not possible to send a very definite reply." [251]

251 "Fred Ward Buys Clothes; Sustains Burns at Farm. Work Farm Superintendent, Reported Among Missing, Turns up Smiling in New Suit," *Duluth News*

## Flora (Witte) Wargin and Nick Wargin

**(Flora-12-1-1891 to 9-12-1982; Nick – 12-5-1886 to 8-6-1950)**

One of my mother's paternal aunts, Flora (Witte) Wargin, and her husband, Nicholas, survived the Fires by running to their freshly plowed field and lying flat in the plowed furrows until after the Fires had passed. Their farm was located just across the border between Hermantown and Canosia Townships. In 1918 they had one child with them: Frances, who was born October 4, 1915.

## Four Unnamed Hermantown Families

A letter sent to the editor from a woman named Ida Josephine Watson was published in the Duluth News Tribune of November 19, 1918. She wrote about her appreciation for the Henry Bridgeman family, who sheltered Ida and her family in their home as well as four unidentified Hermantown families. This was illustrative of many of the residents of Superior, Carlton, and Duluth, who welcomed fire refugees into the safety of their homes.

"Tribute to Mr. and Mrs. Henry Bridgeman. *To the Editor of the News Tribune:* If you will kindly print the enclosed you will oblige. Yours respectfully, IDA JOSEPHINE WATSON, Duluth.

"Among the many great kindnesses shown near and actual fire victims last Saturday night, I want to acknowledge that of Mr. and Mrs. Henry Bridgeman and family. A group of residents of Fortieth Avenue East had left their homes and started down the avenue for the lake shore as the nearest place of safety, but finding the 50-mile gale laden with dense smoke and cinders too much to battle against, they crouched together, on the gold links-which border Fortieth Avenue—and there held a council of war as to the best course to take to insure their safety. A mother and two little children-one in arms and the other 2 years of age-had joined the group. They had been there a short time when the Northland Country Club house burst into flames adding immense burning cinders to the furious onrushing wind. One of the group decided then they must move at once-but how and where was the tragic question. Many automobiles had torn down the avenue filled with people fleeing for safety. When our problem was most acute and still unsolved-a large car came down Fortieth Avenue, stopped and a voice called, "Come quickly: everyone get in." It didn't take long! In an instant mother, children and all were being driven over Fortieth avenue and east on London Road. It was not, however, until we reached his residence that we realized it was Mr. Bridgeman who had rescued us. And we were not the only ones to whom he had given shelter and hope, for his house was filled with people from far and near. Four families from Hermantown were there, beside dozens of others, all being ministered to by the thoughtful attentions of Mr. and Mrs. Bridgeman. Their attentions will never be forgotten and can never be repaid except in the deep appreciation of those who shared their great kindness and tender hospitality."[252]

## The Wentzlaff Family

At the Harvest Fest on September 7, 2013, I was told by a family member that the family stayed and fought the fire, saving the house, barns, and the rather large chicken coop to the north of the house, where they all stayed temporarily. That house is still standing today, near the intersection of Maple Grove and Midway Road.

---

*Tribune*, October 16, 1918. Online at GenealogyBank.com. http://www.genealogybank.com/gbnk/newspapers/doc.

252 Ida Josephine Watson, "Tribute to Mr. and Mrs. Henry Bridgeman," in a Letter to the Editor, *Duluth News Tribune*, November 19, 1918. Online at GenealogyBank.com. http://www.genealogybank.com/doc/newspapers/image.

The original house had burned down ten years earlier, in 1908, according to an article in the Duluth Evening Herald. Fortunately, the entire family, consisting of Mr. Wentzlaff, his wife and five young daughters, as well as Miss Fanny Holden, a Hermantown School teacher who was living with them, did not perish. They did suffer severe frost-bite in their run to a house one-half mile away, as they fled for their lives in their night clothes on a frigid January morning. The house and contents were totally destroyed, and Mr. Wentzlaff had no insurance. I can only imagine how fortunate they felt to not lose their house ten years later, in the 1918 Fires!

## Dorothy Steinle Westberg (March 3, 1911 to March 12, 1990)
### And Sheldon Westberg (1908 to July, 1984)

A nine year old Sheldon Westberg remembered an indignity he had to endure following the Fires, as related by his wife, Dorothy Steinle Westberg.

*"My husband, Sheldon Westberg was about 9 years old when the 1918 forest fire came through Hermantown. Their farm was completely destroyed. He said the Red Cross gave them temporary shelter and clothes while they re-built their farmhouse. He still remembers the girl's button shoes he had to wear to Garfield School that winter."*[253]

## Dagmar Ann Westin (Mrs. Willis Michler)
### (August 6, 1911 to May 13, 2003)

Dagmar Westin lived in the Duluth Heights, on Locust Street, not too far from the Herman Township limits. Her vivid memories of the Fires are recorded for posterity.

Where she lived with her parents, (Lars) Louis Westin, and Hannah (Skoog) Westin, was not too far from the water tower. She remembered watching the smoke all through the day outside, and that her hair was full of smoke and ashes as she ran back and forth on the dirt road in front of their house. The fire neared them, and she remembered the virtual firestorm, with the strong and gusty winds lifting trees and burning masses, throwing them through the sky and then slamming the burning debris down to the ground, in a random fashion. Her father, who was a city of Duluth water and light foreman, made many trips with his truck, taking people on the Howard Gnesen Road to the safety of Duluth. People stood along the road, she said, and her father picked them up. Finally, he came home to rescue his own family. Where they lived in the Heights they were told they were in danger and had to go. Her mother carried a bundle on her back, and her father grabbed his canvas hunting rucksack. The documents, such as the title to their property, were to be taken by her mother. However, in the excitement her mother forgot the legal documents and grabbed photographs of her mother, father, sisters, and other family members.

The Home Guards were racing about, in their Army trucks, rescuing people. She and her family were picked up where a business known as the Highland Garage used to be. In the vicinity of Locust Street and Arlington Avenue she remembered that it was very dark. The sky was glowing in the distance, and then suddenly flames would soar into the sky. The air was so thick with ashes that it was difficult to breathe.

If the wind hadn't shifted, Duluth itself would have burned, she said. (Presumably the wind came out of the east, off Lake Superior.) If the Fire would have advanced down the hillside, there were plans to haul people in trains to Superior, she remembered her father telling her mother.

As they went down Mesaba Avenue, she remembered people standing along the road, yelling, "We've got room for a

253 Dorothy Steinle Westberg, "My Life in Hermantown," unpublished manuscript on file at the Hermantown History Center.

family of four," and similar things. Everybody was offering what shelter they could to the refugees. However, she had an uncle who lived on one of the streets off Mesaba Avenue with whom they stayed.

The next day they went back to their home, with a great deal of trepidation, which turned to elation when they saw that their house was still standing. Later on they drove up Miller Trunk, to the vicinity of Jackson's Corner. There they saw carcasses of burned horses. She remembered a particularly unfortunate horse that was already swollen, legs up in the air, with raw flesh showing beneath his burned hair. A pig farm was not too far away, and there were burned, dead pigs laying everywhere. She remembered that it smelled like roast pork there.

Dagmar said that the inhalation of smoke and ashes killed more people than the actual flames. People's lungs took in all the smoke and ashes, they became ill and all too often died from pneumonia, she opined. Then too, many people took refuge in water, which was cold, for hours. They then got terrible chills and horrible colds.

She remembered that it was "so ugly" after the Fires. There were endless miles of charred trees, hanging everywhere, ready to fall at a moment's notice. Everything was black – "black everywhere." To add to the black ugliness, the Red Cross fire shacks were covered with ugly black tarpaper, amid the black ruins of forests.

In her mind, fireweed belongs to the days of the 1918 Fires. It covered everything the year after, and softened the harsh ugliness of the blackened landscape. That following year she remembered riding with her parents on Miller Trunk, over the Cloquet River Bridge, and seeing nothing but ugly blackness. She plaintively asked her mother, "Do you think I'll live so long that I'll ever see green again?"

There were lots of raspberries for years afterward. However, walking to pick them was difficult, because there were stumps and fallen trees everywhere.[254]

## Marian Canning Whittles

**1914 to December 8, 1918**

On the lists of known injured in the 1918 Duluth newspapers I've seen this surname, listed as being a Hermantown resident. The name was not familiar to me. However, I subsequently learned that the Thomas and Laura Whittles family from which little Marian hailed was a distinguished one. Furthermore, it appears that the family actually resided in Canosia Township, very close to the Herman Township border.

"Dr. Whittles, who has been filling the pulpit at Second Presbyterian Church, 1515 West Superior Street, since the departure for France of Rev. J. A. McCaughey, former pastor of the church, is one of the fire sufferers. Dr. Whittles' wife and little daughter and his parents are all at St. Luke's Hospital receiving treatment for injuries received during the fire. The entire family spent the greater part of the night of the fire in an old well on their place which is about two miles north of the Jackson School."

Other articles from the summer of 1918 describe him as a noted American author and minister, as well as representative of the board in charge of missionary work in the logging camps in Northern Minnesota. [255]

Kathryn Adams gives some additional information on Dr. Whittles and his family. He rescued some people with his car, but on a return trip into the fire area, the engine failed. It was at that point he and his family sought shelter in a well. Injuries sustained in the Fires led to the deaths of his mother and his daughter.[256]

---

254Dagmar Westin Michler, 1918 Fire Remembered, a recorded oral interview of Dagmar Westin Michler, Northeast Minnesota Historical Collections, Archives and Special Collections , Kathryn A. Martin Library, Room 202, University of Minnesota Duluth, 416 Library Drive, Duluth, MN 55812-3001. (S6030)
255"Minister Suffered Burns in the Recent Disaster," *Duluth News Tribune,* October 25, 1918. Online at GenealogyBank.com. http://www.genealogybank.com/doc/newspapers/image.
256 Kathryn Adams & Mary Schrock, "The Forest Fire of 1918," *Canosia Township & Pike Lake: An Illustrated History,* 1988, page 54.

"Funeral services for Marian Canning Whittles, age 4, daughter of Rev. and Mrs. Thomas D. Whittles, who died Friday of burns sustained in the Fires of Oct. 12, were held yesterday afternoon. The family, who reside on Duluth Heights, had a narrow escape the night of the fire." [257]

Marian is buried at Forest Hill Cemetery in Duluth.

## Unknown Author

The following is taken from a chapter in a booklet entitled, "Hermantown: 1874-1976: A History of Hermantown as Remembered by Its Citizens," a copy of which is retained at the Hermantown History Center. Unfortunately, the author is not listed, but presumably is one of the people who contributed to the history booklet of the Booklet Committee of the Hermantown Hockey Auxiliary: Esther Craney; George Erickson; Gladys Erickson; Roy Erickson; Clara Fichtner; Art Nelson; Einar Nelson; Erling Nelson; Ingrid Olson; Helmer Ruth; L. E. Seelig; Ruth Skarp; Mrs. Wagner; and Dorothy Westberg.

*It was a beautiful warm day; more like summer than an autumn day, but very dry.*

*Eleanore Larson and I decided to visit Selma Lindahl who lived near the Albert Anderson farm located about a mile from the Ugstad Road. She was not home, so we walked home leisurely although we made one stop. Recall there was a small fire burning south of the Larson farm. I had planned to heat water after the evening meal for the children's bath, but Uncle did not approve due to the sparks which occasionally came from the chimney might cause a grass fire.*

*He was a very calm person, but as I went outdoors about 7 P.M. the smoke was increasing and I became concerned. I decided to check with our neighbors, the Larsons. Mr. Larson suggested I pack what was important to save, which I did. I recall I ran all the way back and it was dusk. I looked to the northwest and it was burning at that corner of the farm. I told Uncle. His first reaction was to get the cows and horse out of the barn, which he did and closed the doors. I told the children to put on their best clothes and dress their 4-year-old brother. Uncle had told us to go to the root cellar. I sent the children ahead as I was salvaging what I could, so was last to leave the house.*

*I reached the root cellar. Although there was only a little space, due to the large space used for potatoes and other root vegetables. In addition to us, some people had come from Canosia so the space was crowded.*

*We were not there very long, as due to the strong wind pieces of burning wood were coming through the opening at the rear, used for a wooden trough to get the vegetables in the bins, so we had to leave the cellar. There was a large rock pile and Uncle told us to lie on the ground beneath it which we did.*

*Uncles' sister, Mrs. Boquist, and Mr. Hansen had left their homes in Canosia and Mrs. Jorgen Erickson went over to Uncle's farm and we located them and Mrs. Boquist in a ditch west of the root house. When we felt it safe to look around we noticed a small chicken coop on the J. C. Erickson farm. We decided to get out of the wind as none of us had sweaters on. We entered the chicken coop, only one or two in there, but not for long as the headlights of a car appeared. It had a driver and a Boy Scout as an assistant to rescue fire victims. Mrs. Erickson and son and daughter and I and the four cousins were taken to the Armory in Duluth. The Red Cross women were there to minister to the fire victims. They had cots set up on the second floor where we spent the night. We were unaware there were so many there until we were served breakfast on the first floor. What a pitiful sight we saw! Many people were bandaged, having sustained burns. I recall I had difficulty eating and being so grateful we had escaped unharmed, but concerned for those we saw. The Red Cross inquired if we had someone in town where we could stay. They must have provided the carfare for our transportation to the West End where our Aunt and Uncle lived. They moved from their farm in Canosia in the spring of 1918. Their home and other buildings were also destroyed.*

257 "Funeral of Marian Whittles Held: Was Victim of Fire," *Duluth News Tribune*, December 8, 1918. Online at GenealogyBank.com. http://www.genealogybank.com/doc/newspapers/image.

*The Brinteson family and Mrs. Boquist were given a temporary home at the A. Borgens, a relative in Duluth. Uncle and Mr. Boquist rebuilt the Mr. B. home in Canosia and the Brinteson family lived there and attended the Canosia School, which did not burn. There were a number of friends and others we knew who died as a result of the fire, others perished at their homes and en route to Duluth.*

*The family returned to their new home when finished in 1919. I remained in Duluth and while there, Fred Ward, Superintendent of the County Work farm called me and asked if I would like to come and live with them and assist Mrs. Ward. I stayed there until October, 1919, when Betsy Ugstad and I traveled to Kansas City. I returned to Duluth in 1920.*[258]

## Hermantown Deaths

It may never be known exactly how many people died in the months after the Fires. As has been previously stated here, a considerable number of Hermantown residents who died as direct result of the fire but survived long enough to be taken to Duluth hospitals were not recorded in the township records.[259] In the frenzied aftermath of the Fires, incorrect information was inadvertently recorded as to both the spelling of the names of the victims as well as their area of residence. Over a period of years the names of Hermantown area victims have been compiled and researched by Sandra Reinke, Bette Grussendorf, Delaine Carlson, and others of the Hermantown Historical Society.

According to Franklin R. Raiter and Francis M. Carroll, 453 people were killed in the entire fires area, and another 106 people were killed by influenza and pneumonia that struck the weakened immune systems of the survivors after the Fires. More than 2,000 were injured; 52,371 refugees had their homes, property, and livelihoods swept away in the flames.[260]

1. **Edward Anderson,** 14 or 15 years old;
2. **Louis Archambault**, 90 years old;
3. **Frank Henry Berglund,** 2 years old, Maple Grove Road;
4. **Marie Charlotte Erickson,** 17 months;
5. **Mildred Halverson**, 15 years old;
6. **Myrna Halverson,** 17 years old;
7. **Aino Hatinen,** 2 ½ years of age
8. **Aurora Janzig,** 6 years;
9. **Anton Klosowsky,** 75 years;
10. **Amelia Klosowsky,** 66 years;
11. **Mrs. Mary LaCourse,** 62 years old;
12. **Nikolai Larson,** age 59, Maple Grove Road;
13. **Edwin Lawyer Jr.**, 9 years;
14. **Edwin Lawyer,** 63 years old;
15. **Ida (Mrs. Edwin) Lawyer,** 60 years old;
16. **Anna Peterson (Mrs. Fred Peterson)** of Adolph, 67 years old.

258 "Hermantown, 1874-1976. A History of Hermantown as Remembered by Its Citizens," published by Booklet Committee of the Hermantown Hockey Auxiliary.

259 Arthur Fichtner, et. al,"Hermantown, 1874-1976. A History of Hermantown as Remembered by its Citizens," printed by Booklet Committee of the Hermantown Hockey Auxiliary. (Quote by Arthur Fichtner.)

260 Francis M. Carroll and Franklin R. Raiter,"The People Versus the Government: The 1918 Cloquet Fire and the Struggle for Compensation," *Journal of Forest History,* Vol. 29, No. 1 (Jan., 1985) page 4, Published by Oxford University Press on behalf of Forest History Society and American Society for Environmental History. Stable URL: http://www.jstor.org/stable/4004968. Accessed: December 9, 2017.

A few others sometimes mentioned as Hermantown casualties appear to be from other areas. Two young children, Violet (born in 1913) and Edward Archambeau, (born in 1915) were from Duluth, and perished on the Hutchinson Road. The "Falitier" family of Adolph was probably a misspelling for Pelletier, and they were probably from adjoining Solway Township. Lucenda Jordan, age 66, did not reside in Hermantown, and was probably working for a family at their Pike Lake cabin. Herman Diedrich is also sometimes listed as a Hermantown casualty, but upon further investigation he was actually from nearby Midway Township. Another casualty was listed as 10 year old Myrtle Helen Ekstrand, who died near the Maple Grove Road, on October 12, 1918. However, she and her parents, Nels Ekstrand and Hulda Olson Ekstrand, appear in census records to have been from Proctor rather than Hermantown. Perhaps she was visiting somebody in Hermantown on the Maple Grove Road at the time of her death.

# III. Addenda

## ADDENDUM I

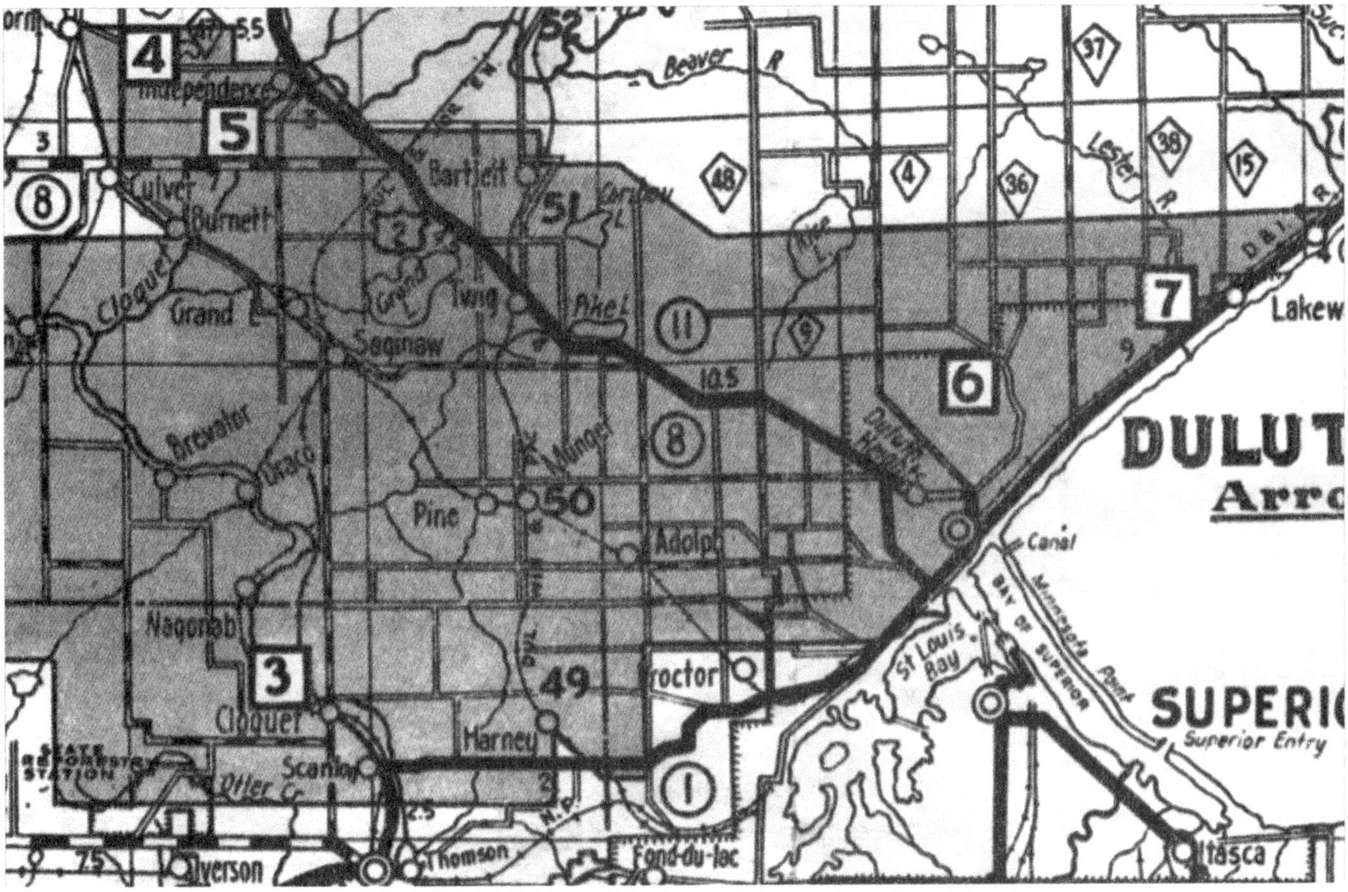


Darkened areas are approximate areas the 1918 Fires burned in the Hermantown vicinity. Note that the immediate shoreline of Duluth was mostly spared, except for the area by the Northland Country Club. Map is cropped from larger map from booklet, "A Brief Statement of Facts," by the Minnesota Forest Fires Reimbursement Association 1918, by Northern Printery Press, Cloquet.(Undated)

# ADDENDUM II

## Duluth and The Extent of Fires There

Although parts of Duluth did burn and the city was ringed by fire, most of the city was spared. It was suggested that Duluth was saved by the rocky hills paralleling the shores of Lake Superior and the St. Louis River Bay, as well as an easterly breeze that developed shortly after 2 A.M.on the 13th.[261] The Fires reached Lake Superior, burning across Lakewood, Lakeside, and Lester Park, as well as a large part of the Woodland area. One of the easternmost properties destroyed by the Fire was the farm of Theodore Hollister. The Northern Pacific Railroad sent a relief train to Lakeside on the Duluth and Iron Range track to bring people to what was hoped to be the safety of Duluth. Elizabeth Bachman, who wrote the History of Forestry in Minnesota, speculated that the Fires were kept out of western Duluth by volunteers around the Nopeming Sanatorium community and grounds that brought the fire there under control. Also, she noted that for most of the length of the city troops of the Duluth Fire Department, volunteers, and Home Guards members put out spot fires, to keep the fires out of the rest of Duluth.[262] In western Duluth bursts of heat and flame kindled fires in the Northern Pacific Railway's yard. The Alger-Smith Lumber Company caught fire on Rice's Point. Sparks and firebrands from the lumberyard fire ignited the Interstate Bridge between Duluth and Superior, rendering about two thousand feet of the Great Northern Railway Bridge between Duluth and Superior out of operation for a month.[263]

---

261 J.R. Lloyd, "The Forest Weather Service in the Lake States, " *Monthly Weather Review* Weather Bureau, Chicago Ill, January, 1931, page. 31. https://docs.lib.noaa.gov.rescue.mwr.059-mwr.
262 Ken Jackson, "Fires Above Duluth," The Fire Trail," http:www.cpinternet.com/~kjackson/fire/jffiresduluth.html. Accessed 1-20-2004.
263 *Ibid.*

# ADDENDUM III

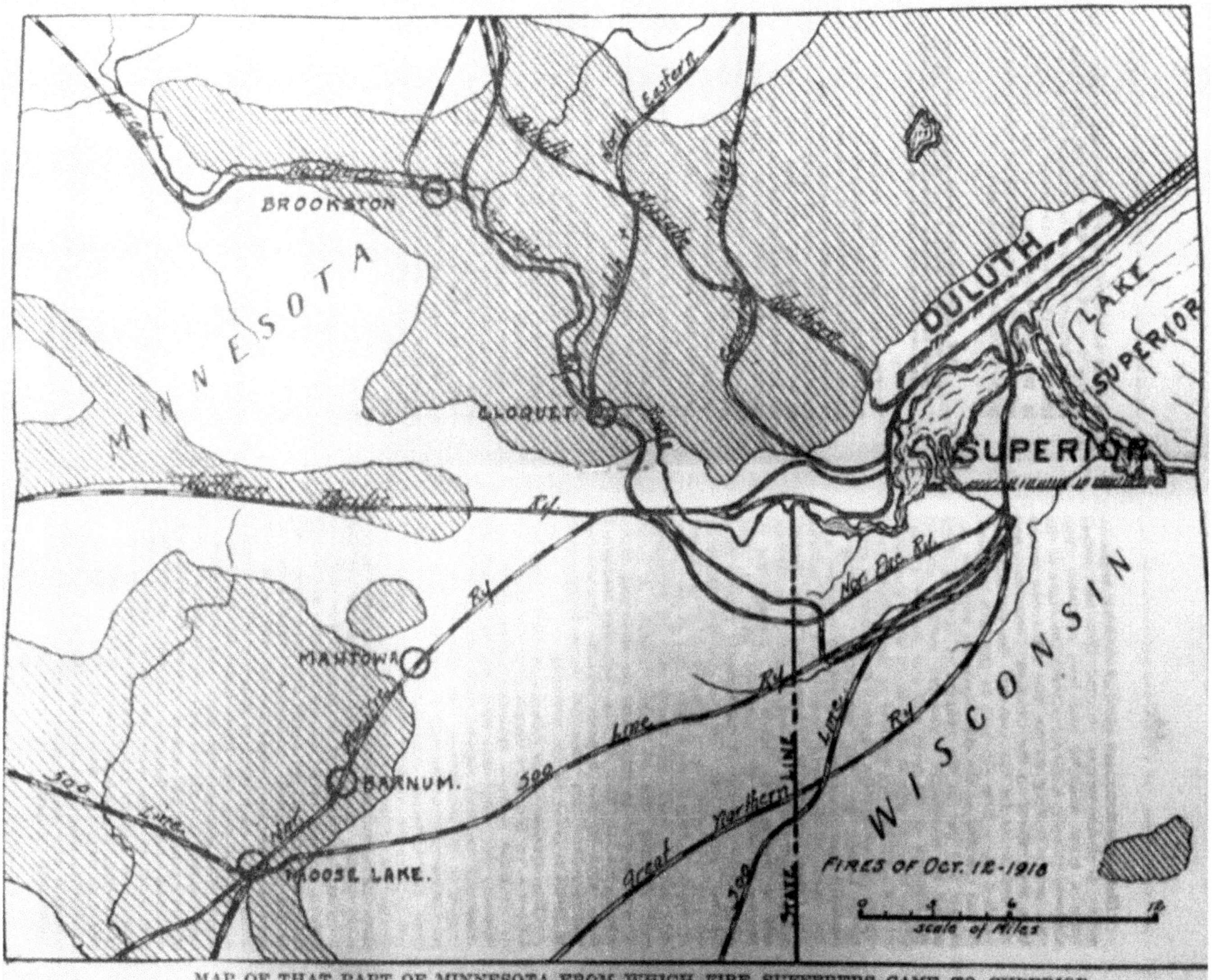


MAP OF THAT PART OF MINNESOTA FROM WHICH FIRE SUFFERERS CAME TO SUPERIOR.

264

Map from pamphlet titled, "Report to Donors," by the Superior Relief Committee, Superior, Wis. Northeastern Minnesota Forest Fires of October 12, 1918, dated November 1, 1919. It shows an approximate area of burned areas, with railroads inserted.

264 1918 Forest Fire Documents, Item 1: *Report to Donors,* published report by Superior Relief Committee, Northeast Minnesota Historical Collections, Archives and Special Collections, Kathryn A. Martin Library, University of Minnesota Duluth.

# ADDENDA IV

## (Wrongful Death Court Order of Louis Archambault)

No.51184

STATE OF MINNESOTA DISTRICT COURT

COUNTY OF ST.LOUIS ELEVENTH JUDICIAL DISTRICT

Probate Court

File 12163

Edmund Archambeau, Administrator of )
The estate of Lewis Archambeau, deceased, )
Plaintiff, )
-vs- )
)
James G.Davis, As Agent of the President )
Under The Transportation Act of 1920, )
Defendant. )
)

The above entitled cause came on for hearing before the Court on October 8, 1941, at the County Court House in the City of Duluth, Minnesota, pursuant to an order duly made by the Court, upon a petition for supplemental distribution of funds received on account of the wrongful death of decedent above named; there was no other appearance in said proceeding.

Due proof of the service of said order for hearing as therein provided having been submitted, and sufficient and satisfactory evidence having been offered and received in support of said petition, and as to the heirs, next of kin, and persons entitled to receive said funds after the payment of expenses, and the Court being fully advised in the premises,

The Court finds that decedent Lewis [sic] Archambeau lost his life in the great fire of October 12, 1918; that The City National Bank of Duluth as administrator of his estate has now recovered from the United States Government the sum of $120.00 as balance of the damages arising out of said death; and that at the time of his said death the next of kin of said Lewis [sic] Archambeau were his eight children, namely, Edmund Archambault, son; Amede Archambault, son; Felix Archambault, son; Mevlina Krause, daughter; Anne Pelletier, daughter; Minnie Boire, daughter; Emma Becotte, daughter; and Louis Archambault, son, who are the sole and only persons entitled to share in said fund.

The Court further finds that since the death of Lewis [sic] Archambeau his three sons Amede Archambault, Felix Archambault and Louis Archambault have died and Amede Archambault's estate has been probated and the final decree of the Probate Court of St.Louis County, Minnesota, assigned all of his estate to his sole surviving daughter, Alma Babcock.The Court has insufficient information to determine the distributees of the shares of Felix Archambault and Louis Archambault.

IT IS THEREFORE ORDERED, That The City National Bank of Duluth, as representative of said estate, distribute the sum of $120.00 so recovered on account of the wrongful death of said decedent, as follows:

(1) Lathers & Hoag, for expenses incurred and to be incurred: $2.50
(2) The City National Bank of Duluth, as compensation for services and for Expenses in this proceeding: $15.00
(3) Lathers & Hoag, as compensation, exclusively for services in the Proceeding for distribution and discharge of petitioner: $20.00
(4) That said representative endorse and deliver to Theodore Hollister, et.al., The warrant of the United States for $12.00
(5) Edmund Archambeau, son of decedent: $8.81
(6) Alma Babcock, daughter and sole heir of Amede Archambault, deceased Son of decedent: $8.81
(7) Melvina Krause, daughter of decedent: $8.82
(8) Anne Pelletier, daughter of decedent: $8.82
(9) Minnie Boire, daughter of decedent: $8.81
(10) Emma Becotte, daughter of decedent: $8.81
(11) Pay in to the Clerk of District Court of St.Louis County, Minnesota for The persons entitled thereto, subject to the further of the Court, the Shares of Felix Archambault and Louis Archambault, deceased sons of Decedent. $17.62

$120.00

IT IS FURTHER ORDERED, That said representative proceed with due diligence to make such distribution pursuant to this Order and that it file receipts for such payments made hereunder in the office of the Clerk of this Court at the Court House in Duluth, Minnesota, or with the Judge of Probate Court of St. Louis County, Minnesota.

AND IT IS FURTHER ORDERED, That upon complying with this Order plaintiff may without giving notice, apply for an Order of the Probate Court of St .Louis County, Minnesota, releasing and discharging it from all liability, if any, for any matters relating to the above entitled matter.

Dated the 10th day of November, 1941.

E.J.Kenny
Judge of District Court
St. Louis County, Minn.

FILED IN MY OFFICE AT
Nov 14 1941
FRED ASH, Clerk of Dist. Court
By J. H. Moon, Deputy [265]

*[Court form retyped from microfilm at St. Louis County Courthouse, Duluth, by author, to facilitate reading.]*

265 Op.cit., retyped by Connie Jacobson from microfilm.

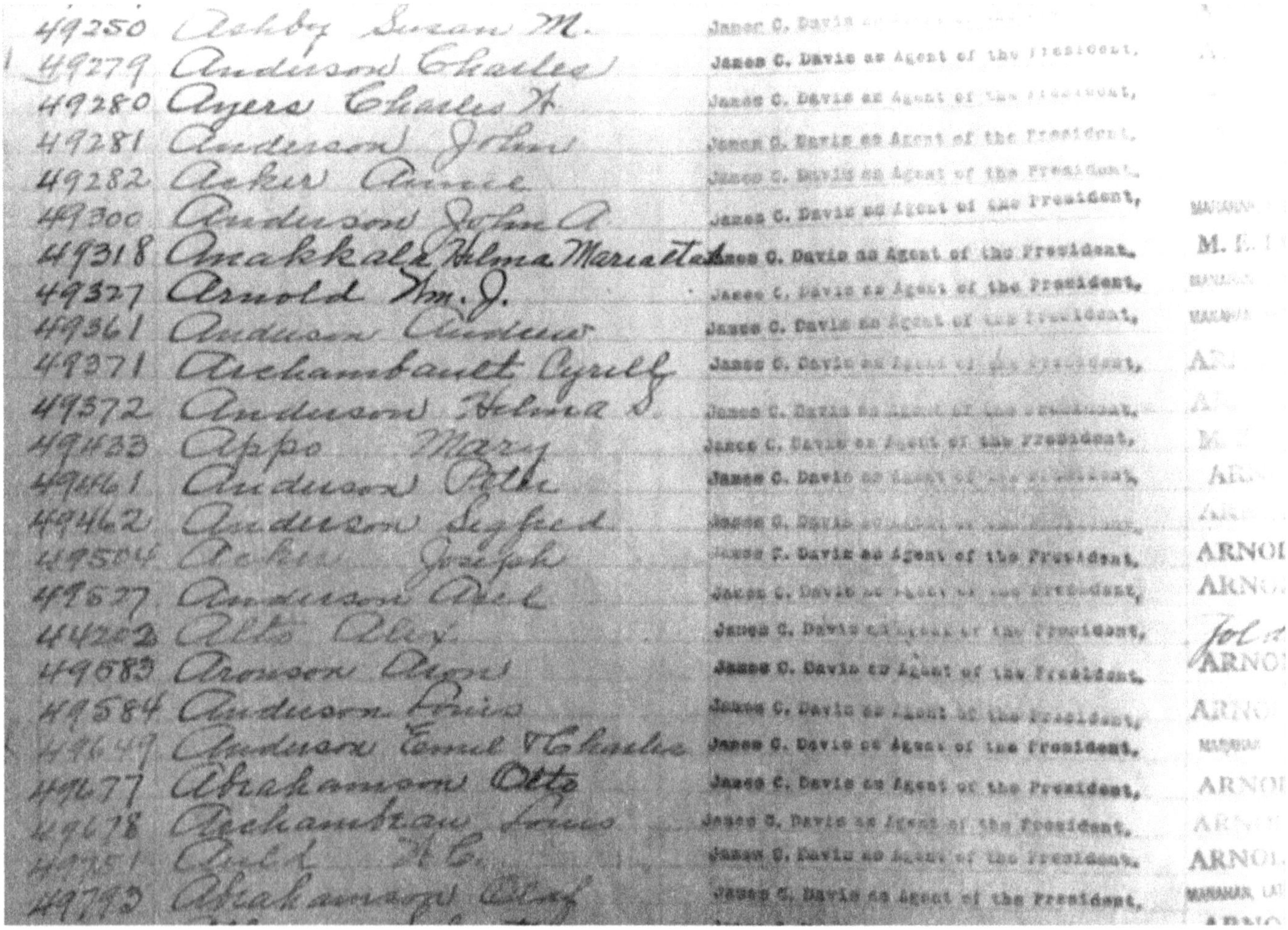

| | | |
|---|---|---|
| 49250 | Ashby Susan M. | James C. Davis |
| 49279 | Anderson Charles | James C. Davis as Agent of the President, |
| 49280 | Ayers Charles H. | James C. Davis as Agent of the President, |
| 49281 | Anderson John | James C. Davis as Agent of the President, |
| 49282 | Acker Annie | James C. Davis as Agent of the President, |
| 49300 | Anderson John A | James C. Davis as Agent of the President, |
| 49318 | Anakkala Helma Mariatta | James C. Davis as Agent of the President, |
| 49327 | Arnold Wm. J. | James C. Davis as Agent of the President, |
| 49361 | Anderson Andrew | James C. Davis as Agent of the President, |
| 49371 | Archambault Cyril | James C. Davis as Agent of the President, |
| 49372 | Anderson Helma S. | James C. Davis as Agent of the President, |
| 49433 | Appo Mary | James C. Davis as Agent of the President, |
| 49461 | Anderson Pelle | James C. Davis as Agent of the President, |
| 49462 | Anderson Sigfred | James C. Davis as Agent of the President, |
| 49504 | Acker Joseph | James C. Davis as Agent of the President, |
| 49577 | Anderson Axel | James C. Davis as Agent of the President, |
| 49582 | Alto Alex | James C. Davis as Agent of the President, |
| 49583 | Aronson Agnes | James C. Davis as Agent of the President, |
| 49584 | Anderson Louis | James C. Davis as Agent of the President, |
| 49647 | Anderson Emil & Charles | James C. Davis as Agent of the President, |
| 49677 | Abrahamson Otto | James C. Davis as Agent of the President, |
| 49678 | Archambeau Louis | James C. Davis as Agent of the President, |
| 49751 | Auld H. C. | James C. Davis as Agent of the President, |
| 49793 | Abrahamson Alex | James C. Davis as Agent of the President, |

The above is a copy of a portion of one of three large books containing judgments resulting from the 1918 Fires as filed in St. Louis County Court. Louis Archambeau [sic.] has judgment number 49678, with judgment against James C. Davis as Agent of the President, filed by the Duluth law firm of Arnold and Arnold. The Judgment books are filed in the Special Collections Archives of the Kathryn A. Martin Library at UMD, Box 51, vol.2.[266]

266 St. Louis County District Court selected records (Judgment book), Northeast Minnesota Historical Center Collections, Archives and Special Collections, Kathryn A. Martin Library, University of Minnesota Duluth. (S2253)

# ADDENDA V
# (Verified Claim Against USA Railroad Admin.)

Several pages of form, courtesy of Delaine Carlson (Referred to in Alice Walin Item.)

125

Zone #2

COPY

Claim No.

DO NOT FILL IN

NAME OF CLAIMANT | LOCATION OF PROPERTY | RAILROADS INVOLVED

**VERIFIED CLAIM**
**AGAINST**
**UNITED STATES OF AMERICA**
**RAILROAD ADMINISTRATION**

**FOR PROPERTY DAMAGE FROM FIRES OF**
**OCTOBER 12, 1918.**
(Does not include personal injury or death)

**TO BE MADE OUT IN DUPLICATE**

One original must be signed and sworn to before Notary Public
Copy must be complete including all signatures.

Name of Claimant (Print) Emil Johnson
First name in full name. Initial. Last name in full.

Address of Claimant R 1 Box 15A Duluth, Minn
Street and Number. Post Office. State.

Locality where damage sustained Sec 11 Twp 50, Range 15.
Give City, Village or Government Subdivision.

Total Damage Sustained.

Real Estate $ 9368.60

Personal Property $ 8449.00

Total Loss $17817 60

FASTEN SCHEDULES INSIDE PINNING OR STAPLING TH... THIS SPACE.

**THESE CLAIMS WILL BE CAREFULLY INVESTIGATED AND IF EXAGGERATION OR FRAUD IS FOUND OFFENDERS WILL BE REPORTED TO U. S. DEPARTMENT OF JUSTICE UNDER FOLLOWING FEDERAL STATUTES:**

**Section 5438 U. S. Revised Statutes Amended October 23, 1918:**

"Whoever shall make or cause to be made or present or cause to be presented, for payment or approval, to or by any person or officer in the civil, military, or naval service of the United States, or any department thereof ___ any claim upon or against the Government of the United States, or any department or officer thereof ___ knowing such claim to be false, fictitious, or fraudulent; or whoever, for the purpose of obtaining or aiding to obtain the payment or approval of such claim, or for the purpose and with the intent of cheating and swindling or defrauding the Government of the United States, or any department thereof shall ___ make or cause to be made or used, any false ___ voucher account, claim, certificate, affidavit or deposition, knowing the same to contain any fraudulent or fictitious statement or entry; ___ shall be fined not more than $10,000.00 or imprisoned not more than ten years, or both."

## INSTRUCTIONS

1. This claim must be filed in DUPLICATE, (original and one exact copy).

2. EVERY BLANK MUST BE FILLED IN AND EVERY QUESTION ANSWERED, use the words, "None" or "No" where applicable, but do not leave any matter unanswered.

3. Each attached sheet, *must be signed by the claimant* and firmly attached INSIDE these cover pages. Staple or pin through left hand margin in space indicated.

4. Figures given are to be total loss sustained by claimant; not any percentage of the loss.

5. Use typewriter or ink in filling out claim; the use of typewriter will facilitate checking and hasten adjustment; all words and figures must be legible.

6. CLAIMS NOT CORRECTLY MADE OUT WILL BE RETURNED WITHOUT INVESTIGATION, and subsequent claims received before corrected claim is received will be assigned earlier numbers and investigated first.

7. PERSONAL PROPERTY SCHEDULES.- If any property described was situated elsewhere than at the residence or place of business of claimant, give location and brief description of such property on blank sheet of paper, signed by claimant, and attached like other schedules. On articles produced or manufactured by claimant such as grain, cordwood, etc. disregard columns calling for cost and date when new. On all other articles worth ten dollars or more, cost and date when new must be stated, accurately if known. If not known, give as close estimate as possible. Small articles such as silver-ware, table linen, small clothing items, etc., may be grouped with quantity indicated, and cost and year purchased approximated. Where such groups amount to more than $15.00 they must be so itemized as to permit estimate of value by investigators.

8. If insufficient space is provided for any entry, put additional matter together with any other facts affecting claim on blank sheets, sign same and attach inside cover sheet.

## FURTHER INVESTIGATION

Agents of the United Stated Railroad Administration will make further investigation of the claims made herein. Claimant, by filing this claim, agrees, upon request, to answer fully, truthfully and correctly such further questions, and furnish such other information in regard to such matters as he may be able to do. Failure to comply fully with such requests will absolutely prevent adjustment until compliance

## SCHEDULE OF REAL ESTATE LOSS.

**Includes All Damage to (1) Buildings, (2) Standing Timber, (3) Land.**

**A.**

**Description of Real Estate.**

**(Here give legal description of all real estate on which claimant claims damages. Give lot and block, or subdivision, section, town and range.)**

The SE 1/4 of SW 1/4 of Sec 11, Twp 50 Range 15.

**B.**

**Title and Possession**

1. **Was claimant fee owner of all real estate above described on Oct. 12, 1918?** Yes
2. **Was claimant in possession of all or part of said real estate on Oct. 12, 1918? Indicate facts.**

Yes

3. **Was any other person in possession or occupancy of any part of said real estate on Oct. 12, 1918. and, if so, under what agreement, right or claim? Give names and addresses, if known, of any such person.**

No

4. **Did any other person have or make any claim to any interest in said real estate or the buildings, timber, and structures thereon on Oct. 12, 1918? If so state name, address and nature of claim.**

No

5. **What encumbrances (mortgages, contracts for sale, liens, timber deeds, etc.,) were in existence on October 12, 1918, affecting all or part of said lands? Give (1) name of holder, (2) amount unpaid, (3) book and page of record, if any, (4) whether mortgage, lien or other encumbrance. If none, so state. If since satisfied, so state.**

None

FASTEN INSIDE COVER PAGES BY STAPLING OR PINNING THROUGH THIS SPACE

6. Give book and page of record, or, if unrecorded, attach true and complete copy of deed, contract, or other instrument under which claimant held title or possession on October 12, 1918. If under contract, give balance now unpaid and name of owner.

Warranty Deeds dated July 6th, 1905 recorded in Book 229 of Deeds on page 628 Covering SE¼ of SW¼ Section 11 Township 50 Range 15 St. Louis County, Minnesota

C.

**ATTORNEY'S CERTIFICATE.**

The undersigned hereby certifies that he is a duly licensed attorney at law for Minnesota and has made thorough examination of the record title to all the above described real estate; that, as a result of such examination, he is of the opinion that on Oct. 12, 1918 the fee title of record in said premises was in Emil Johnson subject only to the following contracts, leases, encumbrances, agreements, and defects in title (Here set out any such matter with reference to record. If space insufficient, attach rider with signature of attorney.)

No liens or encumbrance

No recorded instrument since said date assigns or purports to assign claimant's right to damages to said real estate from fire on Oct. 12, 1918.

This certificate is made in support of this verified claim for damages against the United States Government, and with the understanding that it will be relied upon by said government in making settlement therefor.

John B. Arnold

Attorney at Law.

THIS SPACE FOR ATTACHING TO COVER SHEETS

# SCHEDULE OF PERSONAL PROPERTY LOSS

**INCLUDES ALL PROPERTY LOSS EXCEPT TO BUILDINGS, STANDING TIMBER AND LAND.**

**SEE INSTRUCTIONS NO. 7. USE AS MANY OF THESE SHEETS AS NECESSARY.**

| | Number or Quantity | Kind and Description | Cost Price When New | Year When New | October 1918 Value | Damage by Fire. | Do Not Fill Out. (To Be Used |
|---|---|---|---|---|---|---|---|
| SAMPLE ENTRIES | 1 | Piano-upright Knabe | $ 300 00 | 1916 | 150 00 | 150 00 | |
| | 10 bu. | Oats | ........ | .... | 5 00 | 5 00 | |
| | 2 doz. | Table Spoons | $ 6 00 | 1910 | 2 00 | 2 00 | |

**ABOVE IS SAMPLE ONLY: START YOUR LIST BELOW.**

| | | | | | | |
|---|---|---|---|---|---|---|
| 1 | Leather Uph Chair | 12 00 | 1912 | 10 00 | 10 00 | |
| 1 | Leather Uph Rocker | 12 00 | 1912 | 10 00 | 10 00 | |
| 1 | Leather Uph Davenport | 20 00 | 1912 | 20 00 | 20 00 | |
| 1 | Morris Chair | 12 00 | 1912 | 10 00 | 10 00 | |
| 1 | Marble Top Library Table | 25 00 | 1910 | 20 00 | 20 00 | |
| 1 | 9x12 Rug | 60 00 | 1917 | 50 00 | 50 00 | |
| 1 | Family Portrait | 25 00 | 1908 | 25 00 | 25 00 | |
| 1 | Center Table | 20 00 | 1915 | 15 00 | 15 00 | |
| 1 | DRChairs | 3 00 | 1914 | 2 00 | 2 00 | |
| 1 | DRChair | 3 00 | 1914 | 2 00 | 2 00 | |
| 1 | DRChair | 3 00 | 1914 | 2 00 | 2 00 | |
| 1 | DRChair | 3 00 | 1914 | 2 00 | 2 00 | |
| 1 | DRChair | 3 00 | 1914 | 2 00 | 2 00 | |
| 1 | DRChair | 3 00 | 1914 | 2 00 | 2 00 | |
| 1 | 3x6 Rug | 9 00 | 1915 | 6 00 | 6 00 | |
| 1 | 4x8 Rug | 12 00 | 1916 | 8 00 | 8 00 | |
| 1 | Book case | 20 00 | 1912 | 15 00 | 15 00 | |
| 1 | Writing Desk | 35 00 | 1910 | 25 00 | 25 00 | |
| 1 | Sewing Machine | 80 00 | 1900 | 25 00 | 25 00 | |
| 1 | Wall Clock | 15 00 | 1914 | 10 00 | 10 00 | |
| 1 | Picture | 10 00 | 1908 | 10 00 | 10 00 | |

FASTEN INSIDE COVER PAGES STAPLING OR PINNING THROUGH THIS SPACE.

## D. BUILDINGS.

| Use. Dwelling Barn, Store, etc. | Type of Construction, Brick, Frame, Veneer, Log, Stucco, etc. | When Built. Approximate if Unknown. | Number of Stories | Height to Eaves | Oct. 1918 Value | Amount Damage by Fire | Do Not Fill In. (For Use by Investigators) |
|---|---|---|---|---|---|---|---|
| Dwelling | Hewed Logs | 1913 | 1½ | 12' | 3229.40 | 3229 40 | |
| Chicken Coop | Cedar Logs | 1913 | 1 | 8' | 360 | 360 00 | |
| Blacksmith | Frame | 1916 | 1 | 12' | 403.20 | 403 20 | |
| Barn | Hewed Logs | 1915 | 1½ | 15' | 4050 | 4050 00 | |
| Machine & Tool House | Frame | 1916 | 1 | 8' | 1080 | 1080 00 | |

Total Building Damage $122 60

THIS SPACE FOR ATTACHING TO COVER SHEETS

In this space give rough sketch of ground floor of each building showing arrangement of rooms and outside dimensions.

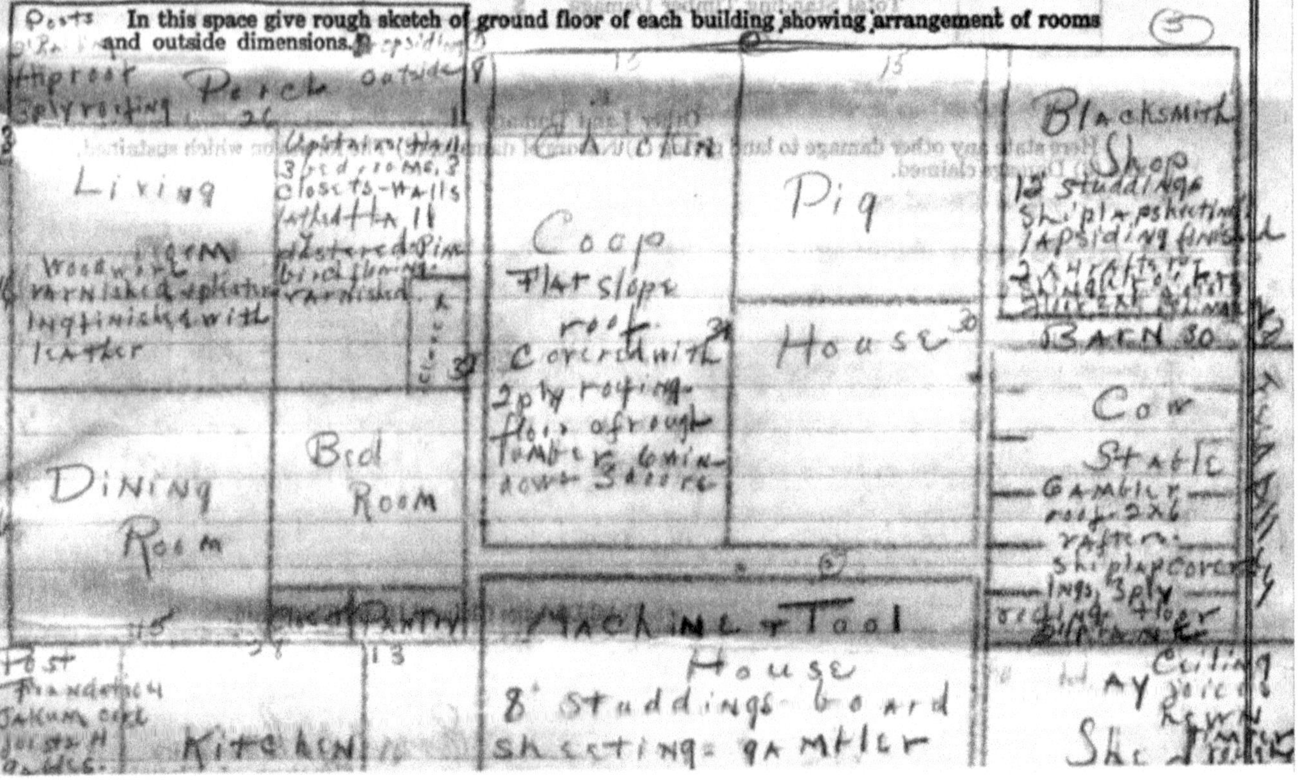

If plumbing, heating, or lighting systems involved, give brief description type, and cost, and date of installation, if known.

None

### E.
### STANDING TIMBER DAMAGE

| Kind of Timber (Birch, Tamarack, etc.) | Use to Which Suited (Ties, Posts, Pulp, etc.) | Quantity Killed By Fire. | Quantity Cut or Sold Since Fire | Forties on Which Situated | Net Damage Claimed | Do Not Fill In. (For Use by Investigators) |
|---|---|---|---|---|---|---|
| None | | | | | | |
| | | | | | | |
| | | | | | | |
| | | | | | | |
| | | | | | | |
| | | | | | | |

Total Standing Timber Damage $

### F.
### Other Land Damage

Here state any other damage to land giving (1) Nature of damage, (2) The forties on which sustained, and (3) Damage claimed.

160' 6' wire fencing 6.00

320 rods 3 wire fencing 240.00

Total Damage Claimed Under This Head. $ 246 00

Emil Johnson

Signature of Clamaint.

**EVERY SHEET MUST BE SIGNED**

## FIRE INSURANCE

The claimant hereby certifies and represents that there was no fire insurance on any property for which claim is hereby made except as shown in the following table:

| Insurance Company | Amount Insurance Paid | Property covered by Insurance. (General Description) |
|---|---|---|
| NW Ins. Co. | $1000.00 | Dwelling |
| | | |
| | | |
| | | |
| | | |

## ATTORNEYS

The Claimant hereby represents that Arnold & Arnold of Duluth Minnesota are his duly authorized attorneys at law to prosecute and settle the claim hereby presented and that no other attorney or lawyer has any contract or agreement, for the prosecution thereof.

## HUSBAND OR WIFE

Is Claimant married? Yes

If so, have spouse execute release below:

## RELEASE OF SPOUSE

In consideration of the investigation, allowance and settlement of the above claim with the above named claimant I the undersigned spouse of said claimant hereby release any claim on my part for any damage to any property above described and agree that payment to claimant of any amount agreed upon with him in settlement of this claim will release all my claim therefor.

VERIFICATION

STATE OF MINNESOTA,
COUNTY OF St. Louis } ss.

Ernest Johnson, being first duly sworn, on oath says (that affiant is the claimant within named) ~~(that affiant is the ... of the within named corporation claimant) (that affiant is one of the co-partners of the within named partnership claimant);~~ that affiant has heard read or read the whole of the forgoing verified claim against the United States, consisting of this cover sheet(4 pages) and 7 additional sheets, each bearing the signature of affiant that the same is in all things true and correct; that all the items of real and personal property therein described were owned by claimant as therein indicated and were destroyed or damaged by the fire of Oct. 12, 1918 and that the values therein stated and the damages therein claimed are correct according to affiants best judgment, information and belief; that all of the answers to questions and the figures and facts therein contained and represented are correct; that claimant actually sustained at least the total amount of damage therein claimed as a direct result of said fire; that said claim is wholly unpaid; that the same has never been assigned; that the same is still the property of claimant; that the signature of claimant's spouse on the preceding page hereof is the genuine signature of said spouse, affixed after affiant had explained to said spouse the meaning thereof.

Subscribed and sworn to before me

Ernie Johnson
Signature of Claimant.

this 25 day of February, 1922.

L. L. Blais

L. L. BLAIS
[NOT]ARY PUBLIC, St. Louis County, Minn.
[My] Commission Expires Oct. 26th, 1926.

INTERPRETER'S OATH

Does Claimant read and understand English thoroughly? Yes

If answer is "No", oath below must be executed.

STATE OF MINNESOTA,
COUNTY OF ______ } ss.

______, being first duly sworn, on oath says that he understands, speaks, and reads both the English and ______ language; that before the foregoing verification was signed by the above named claimant he read over and interpreted the same and the oath administered therewith to said claimant, and read over and interpreted to him all the various figures, questions, items, and statements in the foregoing claim, all in said last named language, with which said claimant is familiar; that affiant believes that when said claimant took said oath he understood and was familiar with all the contents of said claim and verification.

Subscribed and sworn to, before me

______
Signature of Interpreter

this ______ day of ______, 192__

Notary's Stamp and Seal Must Appear On each Affidavit.

FASTEN SCHEDULES INSIDE STAPLING OR PINNING THROUGH THIS SPACE.

# Acknowledgments

There are many individuals and groups to whom I owe a debt of gratitude.

First and foremost, I am extremely grateful to my patient husband, Clarence Sharpe, who has agonized with me over turns of phrases, organization of the book and its sections, as well as calmly putting up with having stacks of files and papers spread all over the house. I am very appreciative of his helpful suggestions and thoughtful questions.

Fellow Hermantown Historical Society members, especially Delaine Carlson, Bette Grussendorf, Sandra Reinke, and Bob Swanstrom, have been extremely helpful locating information in the History Center's files, collecting information, and sharing it with me. Without their assistance this book would not have been possible.

Aimee Brown, Archivist and Curator of the Special Collections, at the Kathryn A. Martin Library at the University of Minnesota Duluth, has been very accommodating in assisting me with my research.

The Website, Genealogybank.com, has been a virtual treasure trove of ephemeral information, giving a glimpse into those dark days of October and thereafter in 1918.

Jason Wilcox of the *Hermantown Star,* the newspaper of the city of Hermantown, has taken time from his full schedule to search through the archives of the *Star* to locate information from previously written articles.

The work of Francis M. Carroll and Franklin R. Raiter, *Fires of Autmun: The Cloquet-Moose Lake Disaster of 1918,* contains the most complete and thoroughly researched account of reconstructive efforts after the Fires. Anybody who desires to learn more about the Fires of 1918 must read their book. Additionally, their excellent Bibliography functions as a review of literature.

Although it is a medium outside of her usual, cover artist Karen B. Holden agreed to my request to design a cover in a charcoal sketch. I am thankful for her straying outside of her usual method of painting in oils and watercolors.

# Artist's Biography

Karen B. Holden ("KBH"), native Duluth artist, paints Minnesota themed art, mostly in oils and acrylics. She does landscapes, lakescapes (especially Lake Superior scenes), florals and still life. Her work can be viewed at www.karensnorthernmnart.com.

# AUTHOR'S BIOGRAPHY

Connie Jacobson lived most of her formative years in Hermantown, Minnesota, where she developed a keen passion for local history. Her interest in history developed while she grew up listening to her parents, grandparents, and their friends reminiscing about their youth, especially the 1918 Forest Fires. She completed her education at the University of Minnesota Duluth as well as the University of Minnesota Twin Cities, and retired from the St. Louis County Court system. In retirement she has been active in local historical societies and contributes articles of local history to the *Hermantown Star* newspaper. She lives in Esko, Minnesota, with three dogs and her husband.

# Bibliography


Bachmann, Elizabeth. *A History of Forestry in Minnesota.* 1965. **www.files.dnr.state.mn.us/forestry/anniversary**

Barr, Edward. "Shackers Eke Out Lonely Life But Stone's Throw From Duluth. How Have Settlers Survived Winter Since Great Fire? Journey into District Answers Query—Paper Board Houses Have Provided Shelter of a Sort—Interview with Refugees.*Duluth News Tribune,* April 6, 1919. Online at GenealogyBank.com.http://genealogybank.com/doc/newspapers/image.

Bailey, Anne Stultz."Wind and Fire, an October Holocaust!" *Duluth Budgeteer Special Edition*, July 18, 1979.

Bergeson, Brady."Interview with Bertil Erickson." *Hermantown Star*, October 5, 1995.

Booklet Committee of the Hermantown Hockey Auxiliary,et. al.,*Hermantown,1874-1976. A History of Hermantown As Remembered by Its Citizens*,Booklet Committee of the Hermantown Hockey Auxiliary,1976.

Brady,Tim."Feature: Fire and Flu. A Fire in Northeastern Minnesota at the Height of the 1918 Flu Pandemic Tested the State's Disaster-Response Mettle."*Minnesota Medicine*, January 2005, minnesotamedicine.com/Past-Issues.

Brown, Daniel James. *Under the Flaming Sky: The Great Hinckley Firestorm of 1894.* Pp. 131-134; 171-173. Harper Perennial, 2006.

Carlson, Delaine (Johnson). E-mail correspondence to author."My Mother's Story of the 1918 Fire."

Carpenter, Richard. "Railroad Signals of the US: Mileposts and Whistle-stops." http://www.railroadsignals.us/support/mileposts/index.htm.

Carroll, Francis M. *Crossroads in Time: A History of Carlton County Minnesota.* Carlton County Historical Society, Cloquet, Minnesota, 1987, p.222.

Carroll, Francis M., and Franklin R. Raiter."At the Time of Our Misfortune. Relief Efforts Following the Cloquet Fire of 1918."*Minnesota Historical Society Magazine,* Fall, 1983, pp.277-281.http://collections.mnhs.org.MNHistoryMagazine/articles/48

Carroll, Francis M., and Franklin R. Raiter. *The Fires of Autumn: The Cloquet-Moose Lake Disaster of 1918.* Minnesota Historical Society Press, 1990.

Carroll, Francis M., and Franklin R. Raiter."The People Versus the Government: The 1918 Cloquet Fire and the Struggle for Compensation."*Journal of Forest History*, vol.29, no.1, Jan.1985, pp.4–19., URL:**http://www.jstor.org/stable/4004968**.

Collene 'Family Finder.'"Photo of site and memorial marker, plus information." *FindAGrave.com,* July 2, 2014.

Erickson, Janelle."The Catastrophic Fire of 1918 Leaves Lasting Impression on Many Area Lives."*Hermantown Star,* August 31, 2001.

Esko Historical Society. Helberg, Davis, editor., *et.al. Esko's Corner: An Illustrated History of Esko & Thomson Township*.X -Presso Books, 2013.

Falk, C. M. "Same Land's been home to family for over 100 years." *Hermantown Star*, July 15, 1993, pp. 3–4.

Fichtner, Arthur. *The History of the Fichtner Farm: A Reference for My Grandsons.* On file at Hermantown History Center, November, 1973.

Foote, Edwin Milton. *A Text-Book of Minor Surgery*. D. Appleton and Company of New York, 1909. Pp.25-29. *Digitized by the Internet Archive in 2007*, www.archive.org.details.textbookolminors.

"Forest History."Chapter 1." ***www.foresthistory.org/ASPNET/Publications/Region/8/History/chap1/Aspx***.

"Forest History Chapter 9."

***www.Foresthistory.org/ASPNET/Publications/CCCforestry/chap9/Htm***.

Haines, Donald A.,and Rodney W.Sando. *Climatic Conditions Preceding Historically Great Fires in the North Central Region.* USDA Forest Research Paper NC-34, 1969.

Heffernan, Jim. "It Was a Day to Remember." *Cooler Near the Lake: Fifty-Two Favorites from Thirty-Four Years of Deadlines."* X-comm, Duluth, Minnesota, Printed in Brainerd, Minnesota, U.S.A., by Bang Printing, 2008, pp.172-174.

Hermantown Board of Township Supervisors Meeting Notes, pages copied by Bette Grussendorf.

*Hermantown Star* staff. "A History of Hermantown." *Hermantown Star: City of Quality Living*, April 1989, p.5.

# Bibliography


*Hermantown Star* staff."Velander's Memories of the Fire of 1918."*Hermantown Star,* August 31, 2001.

Holbrook, Stewart H. "The Story of Cloquet." *Burning an Empire: The Story of American Forest Fires.* The MacMillan Company, 1943, pp.34-45.

Illikainen, Carol. *Firebeast: The Fires of 1918.* Published in 1994 by Moose Lake Area Historical Society, and republished by same in 2016. P.18.

Jackson Farmers' Club. *History of Jackson Farmers' Club.* Unpublished notes retained at Hermantown Historical Society.

Jackson, Ken."Fires Above Duluth."*The Fire Trail,* Ken Jackson, http:www.cpinternet.com/-kjackson/fire/jffiresduluth.html.

Johnson, Lois E."Commemorating the 80th Anniversary of the Fires of 1918."*The Minnesota History Interpreter,* XXVI, no.6, June 1998.

Kohlts, William. E-mail correspondence with author. October 23, 2013.

LaRoque, Ruby (Archambeau)."Cyril and Alvina Archambeau Family," unpublished family history, retained at the Hermantown Historical Society's History Center.

Lloyd, J.R."The Forest Fire-Weather Service in the Lake States."*Monthly Weather Review,* January 1931, p.31, docs.lib.noaa.gov.rescue.mwr.059-mwr.

Lofald, Doris Constance. "October 12, 1918, as I Remember It."1931. Hermantown Historical Society.

Lyman, Herbert."Smoke From Minnesota Forest Fires."*Monthly Weather Review.* November, 1918, p.506.cods.lib.noaa.gov.resue/mwr/046/mwr-046-11-0506.

Martini, Alice. *Klosowsky: The Family Genealogy. The Story of My Grandparents' Life in Minnesota.* Hermantown History Center.

Moose Lake Area Historical Society, et.al.*1918 Fire Stories.* Moose Lake Area Historical Society, 2003.

Pearson, Lucille M. *History of Fredenberg:1887 to 1981,* p.40.

Peterson, Jana."Carlton County Archaeologist Makes His Living Rediscovering the Past."*Duluth News Tribune,* July 6, 2011.

R., Cathy."Photo of grave sites and memorial marker of Aurora Janzig, plus information about her."*FindAGrave.com,* September 19, 2013.

Ravage, Barbara. *Burn Unit: Saving Lives After the Flames.* DaCapo Press, 2004.

Richardson, H. W. "The Northeastern Minnesota Forest Fires of October 12, 1918."*Geographical Review,* Apr.1919.Vol.7, no.4, 1919. *JSTOR.*www.jstor.org/stable/207371.

Reinke, Sandra, and Colleen MacDonald. *The Book of Esther: For Such a Time as This. Based On the Writings of Esther Nelson Hallock.* 2006, pp.51-57.

Sculley, Francis X."Dunkirk in the Minnesota Woods."*Minnesota Sportsman,* pp.56-57.

(Magazine now On-Line)

Spear, Katharine B. "Emergency Work at Armory a Thing of Mercy: Hundreds of Injured Given Attention."*Duluth News Tribune,* October 15, 1918.Online at GenealogyBank.com/doc/newspapers/image. http://www/genealogybank.com/doc/newspapers/image.

Sundquist, Laura (Manske). *Memories of the 1918 Fire.* Copy retained by daughter, Winnie (Sundquist) Gustafson.

Sundquist, Winnie. *Hermantown.* Copy retained by author, of a handwritten paper she wrote for her ninth grade English class.

*Trackin' Back Magazine.*"1918 Fire Remembered." Vol.3, May of 1981,1982, or 1983. Copy retained at Hermantown History Center had part of the last digit of the year obscured.

Ugstad, Evelyn Mabel. "My Recollections," April, 1979. Unpublished manuscript, a copy of which is retained at the Hermantown Historical Society's History Center.

Wagner, Wilmer (Bud)."Wagner's Autobiography: The 1918 Fire." Unpublished paper retained at Hermantown Historical Society.

Westberg, Dorothy Steinle."My Life in Hermantown."Unpublished paper retained at Hermantown Historical Society.

# Bibliography

**From Archives and Special Collections.Kathryn A.Martin Library, Room 202 Library Annex. University of Minnesota Duluth.416 Library Drive.Duluth, MN 55812-3001.**

Gregory, Patricia."Reminiscence of 1918 Fire."2003. Handwritten letter to Nancy Hanson.(S6072)

Michler, Dagmar Westin. "1918 Fire, Remembered by Dagmar Westin Michler."Oral Interview.(S6030)

1918 Forest Fire Documents, Item 1: *Report to Donors,* published report by Superior Relief Committee, Northeast Minnesota Historical Collections, Archives and Special Collections, Kathryn A. Martin Library, University of Minnesota Duluth.(S6057)

1918 Forest Fire Documents, Item 2: Standard Houses and Barns, Archives and Special Collections, Kathryn A. Martin Library, University of Minnesota, Duluth. (S6057).

Weaver, Roger M. *Scrapbook*, "Report from Medical Officer, Captain Arthur H. Collins, Medical Corps, in charge of 3rd Division Minnesota Home Guard to Commanding Officer of Same." Dated October 26, 1918, Northeast Minnesota Historical Center Collections, Archives and Special Collections, Kathryn A. Martin Library, University of Minnesota Duluth. (S3144)

St. Louis County District Court selected records (Judgment book), Northeast Minnesota Historical Center Collections, Archives and Special Collections, Kathryn A. Martin Library, University of Minnesota Duluth. (S2253)

**From Duluth News Tribune, available online at GenealogyBank.Com.**

**http://www.genealogybank.com**

1. "135 Burned at Hospitals; Doors Opened to Poor. Nurses and Convalescents Turn Efforts to Speedy Relief of Injured Refugees," *Duluth News Tribune,* October 15, 1918. Online at GenealogyBank.com http://www.genealogybank.com/doc/newspapers/image.
2. "Additional Refugees Not Previously Reported," *Duluth News Tribune,* October 15, 1918. Online at GenealogyBankl.com. http://www.genealogybank.com/gbnk/newspapers/doc.
3. "Armory Well Organized to Speed Great Relief Task. Innumerable Departments Care for Needs of Afflicted from Burned Cities and Towns," *Duluth News Tribune,* October 15, 1918. Online at GenealogyBank.com. http://www.genealogybank.com/doc/newspapers/image.
4. "Arms of Duluth Open to Victims; First Aid Given. Army Thronged with Patients Cared for by Red Cross Women-Heroic Rescues," *Duluth News Tribune*, October 13, 1918. Online at GenealogyBank.com. http://www.genealogybank.com/doc.newspapers/image.
5. "Baker Offers Bread Supply," *Duluth News Tribune*, October 14, 1918. Online at GenealogyBank.com. http://www.genealogybank.com/doc/newspapers/image.
6. "Brief Private Funerals Held for Fire Dead. Numerous Interments in Duluth Given by Rushed Undertakers. Baby Burned," *Duluth News Tribune,* October 17, 1918. Online at GenealogyBank.com. http://www.genealogy bank.com/gbnk/newspapers/doc.
7. "Charred Embers Only Left in Adolph Munger District," *Duluth News Tribune,* October 15, 1918. Online at GenealogyBank.com. http://www.genealogybank.com/doc/newspapers/image.
8. "Couple Offers House Free to Refugees of Fire," *Duluth News Tribune*, October 14, 1918. Online at GenealogyBank.com. http://www.genealogybank.com/doc/newspapers/image.
9. "Dead Found Lying by Roadside. Hermantown Loss," *Duluth News Tribune,* October 13, 1918. Online at GenealogyBank.com. http://www.genealogbank.com/doc/newspapers/images.
10. "Dogs Stick to Thresholds; Perish While on Duty," *Duluth News Tribune,* October 23, 1918. Online at GenealogyBank.com. http://www.genealogybank.com/doc/newspapers/image.
11. "Dozen Mail Men Suffer Loss of Homes, Stay on Duty, "*Duluth News Tribune,* October 17, 1918. Online at GenealogyBank.Com. http://www.genealogybank.com/doc/newspapers/image.

12. "Epidemic's Gain is Slow; Public Funerals Banner. Only Seven New Cases Reported on October 19th. Ban on Gatherings is Still Effective," *Duluth News Tribune*, October 19, 1918. Online at GenealogyBank.com. http://www.genealogybank.com/doc/newspapers/image.

13. "Fall Festival to Be Resumed. Farmers to Display Fruits and Crops for First Time since 1918 Forest Fires," *Duluth News Tribune*, September 11, 1920, Online at GenealogyBank.com. http://www.genealogybank.com/doc/newspapers/image.

14. "Farmers Club is Organized. Settlers in Town of Herman Form Organization to Promote their Welfare," *Duluth News Tribune*, May 23, 1913. Online at GenealogyBank.com. http://www.genealogybank.com/doc/newspapers/image.

15. "Farmers Pleased with Success of Market," *Duluth News Tribune*, November 17, 1913. Online at GenealogyBank.com. http://www.genealogybank.com/doc/newspapers/image.

16. "Ferry Traffic Between Ports. Street Car Company Joins with Emergency Steamer. Fares Continues Same," *Duluth News Tribune*, October 19, 1918. Online at GenealogyBank.com. http://www.genealogybank.com/gbnk/newspapers/doc.

17. "Finds Wife and Child in Ruins of Their Home. Many Pitiful Tales of Lost Members of Families Disclosed as Death Toll Grows. Pioneer Perishes," *Duluth News Tribune*, October 15, 1918. Online at GenealogyBank.com. http://www.genealogybank.com/gbnk/newspapers/doc

18. "For Sale," *Duluth News Tribune*, November 5, 1914, through November 17, 1914. Online at GenealogyBank.com. http://www.genealogybank.com/doc/newspapers/image.

19. "Fred Ward Buys Clothes; Sustains Burns at Farm. Work Farm Superintendent, Reported Among Missing, Turns up Smiling in New Suit," *Duluth News Tribune*, October 16, 1918. Online at GenealogyBank.com. http://www.genealogybank.com/gbnk/newspapers/doc.

20. "Funeral of Marian Whittles Held: Was Victim of Fire," *Duluth News Tribune*, December 8, 1918. Online at GenealogyBank.com. http://www.genealogybank.com/doc/newspapers/image.

21. "Funerals Go On Day after Day. Duluth Undertaking Rooms are Scenes of almost Continuous Services for Fire Victims," *Duluth News Tribune*, October 19, 1918. Online at GenealogyBank.com. http://www.genealogybank.com/doc/newspapers/image.

22. "Greenhouses are Important in Gardening," *Duluth News Tribune*, October 30, 1909. Online at GenealogyBank.com. http://www.genealogybank.com/gbnk/newspapers/doc.

23. "Hermantown Fire Refuge Sold by County for $500," *Duluth News Tribune*, August 13, 1919. Online at GenealogyBank.com. http://www.genealogybank.com/doc/newspapers/image.

24. "Hermantown Refugee is Dead; Infant Precedes Her," *Duluth News Tribune*, November 17, 1918. Online at GenealogyBank.com. http://www.genealogybank.com/gbnk/newspapers/doc.

25. "Hermantown Victims," *Duluth News Tribune*, October 17, 1918. Online at GenealogyBank.com. http://www.genealogybank.com/gbnk/newspapers/doc

26. Ida Josephine Watson, "Tribute to Mr. and Mrs. Henry Bridgeman," in a Letter to the Editor, *Duluth News Tribune*, November 19, 1918. Online at GenealogyBank.com. http://www.genealogybank.com/doc/newspapers/image.

27. "Klosowsky Funeral," *Duluth News Tribune*, November 8, 1918. Online at GenealogyBank.com. http://www.genealogybank.com/gbnk/newspapers/doc.

28. "Known Dead-Duluth List," *Duluth News Tribune*, October 15, 1918. Online at GenealogyBank.com. http://www.genealogy-bank.com/gbnk/newspapers/doc.

29. "Losses Close to Duluth Appall; Settlers, Farmers Rally After First Shock, Begin Digging Spuds, "*Duluth News Tribune*, October 18, 1918. Online at GenealogyBank.com. http://www.genealogybank.com/gbnk.newspapers/doc.

30. "Mayor Baxter Calls on Superior to Aid Refugees, "*Duluth News Tribune*, October 13, 1918. Online at GenealogyBank.com. http://www.genealogybank.com/doc/newspapers/image.

31. "Minister Suffered Burns in the Recent Disaster," *Duluth News Tribune*, October 25, 1918. Online at GenealogyBank.com http://www.genealogybank.com/doc/newspapers/image.

32. "Mrs. Louise Stahbrodt Dies; Health Affected During Fire," *Duluth News Tribune*, April 15, 1919. Online at GenealogyBank.com. http://www.genealogybank.com/gbnk/newspapers/doc.

# Bibliography


33. "Mrs. Mary Johnson, Pioneer Resident of Duluth, Dead," *Duluth News Tribune*, April 4, 1920. Online at GenealogyBank.com. http://genealogybank.com/gbnk./newspapers/doc

34. "Oil Company Gives Gasoline for Red Cross Service Use," *Duluth News Tribune*, October 14, 1918. Online at GenealogyBank.com. http://www.genealogybank.com/doc/newspapers/image.

35. "Old, Lame and Gray, Refugee Horse Waits for His Master," *Duluth News Tribune*, May 27, 1919. Online at GenealogyBank.com. http://www.genealogybank.com/doc/newspapers/image.

36. "Outfitting Homeless to Start Anew: Children Refugees at Court House Jury Room Nursery," caption from photos, *Duluth News Tribune*, October 16, 1918. Online at GenealogyBank.com. http://www.genealogybank.com/doc/gbml/newspapers/doc.

37. "Proctor Cares for Suffers from Country. Searchers Find Dead and Pitiful Cases of Distress—Courage Shown by Refugees," Duluth *News Tribune*, October 16, 1918. Online at GenealogyBank.com. http://www.genealogybank.com/doc/newspapers/images.

38. "Refugees Registered in Duluth, Read Them and Help Reunite Fire Stricken Families," *Duluth News Tribune*, October 14, 1918, Online at GenealogyBank.com. http://www.genealogybank.com/doc/newspapers/image.

39. "Sees Rainbow. Hopes for Relief from Dry Weather," *Duluth News Tribune*, October 19, 1918. Online at Genealogybank.com. http://www.genealogybank.com/doc/newspapers/image.

40. "Settlers True Blue; Want to Pay for Bonds. Burned Completely Out, Farmer Orders Lumber and Makes Plans to Rebuild," *Duluth News Tribune*, October 16, 1918. Online at GenealogyBank.com. http://www.genealogybank.com/gbnk/newspapers/doc.

41. "Special Carries Food Supply to Fire Refugees," *Duluth News Tribune*, October 14, 1918. Online at GenealogyBank.com. http://www.genealogybank.com/doc/newspapers/image.

42. "State Sends Supply of Fish Free for Refugees," *Duluth News Tribune*, October 19, 1918. Online at GenealogyBank.com. http://www.genealogybank.com/doc/newspapers/image

43. "Strict Discipline Obtains at Armory [sic.]; Beehive hums. Clean Bedding Needed; Refugees Must Register; Cloquet Sends Call for Clothing," Duluth *News Tribune*, October 15, 1918. Online at GenealogyBank.com. http://www.genealogybank.com/gbnk/newspapers/doc.

44. "Sunday Touring Dangerous, Says Motor Officer. Sightseeing in Burned Areas May Bring Loss of Life, Maj. H.JU. Mullin's Warning," *Duluth News Tribune*, October 19, 1918. Online at GenealogyBank.com. http://www.genealogybank.com/doc/newspapers/image.

45. "Superior Rushes Measures For Refugee Relief," *Duluth News Tribune*, October 15, 1918. Online at GeneaolgyBank.com. http:www.genealogybank.com/doc/newspapers/image

46. "Truck Farms Near Duluth. Ed Lawyer, a Grain Elevator Worker, Goes into Gardening and is Successful," *Duluth News Tribune*, July 1, 1911. Online at GeneaologyBank.com. http:www/genealogybank.com/doc/newspapers/image.

47. "Vandal Buyers Made to Desist. Profiteers Stopped in Areas Near Duluth by Prompt Action of Mayor Magney," *Duluth News Tribune*, October 19, 1918. Online at GenealogyBank.com. http://www.genealogybank.com/doc/newspapers/image.

48. "War Veteran is Burned Badly. Fred Bevis, Recuperating from Wounds Received in Battle, at Hospital, a Fire Victim," *Duluth News Tribune*, October 19, 1918. Online at GenealogyBank.com. http://www.genealogybank.com/doc.newspapers/image.

49. "Work Farm Out of Commission. Fire Damage Compels Use of County Jail-Reconstruction Plans Not Yet Made," *Duluth News Tribune*, October 19, 1918. Online at GenealogyBank.com. http://www.genealogybank.com/doc/newspapers/image.

# Index

# Index

# Index

## T



## U

# Index

# List of Illustrations

To order additional copies of

# Hellfire in Hermantown

Contact Savage Press by
visiting our webpage at
www.savpress.com

or see our Savage Press
Facebook page.

Or call
218-391-3070
to place secure credit card orders.

mail@savpress.com

Discounts for bulk orders from groups or educational organizations are available.